The NATIONAL PARKS JOURNAL

PLAN & RECORD YOUR TRIPS TO THE US NATIONAL PARKS

STEFANIE PAYNE

ADAMS MEDIA
NEW YORK   LONDON   TORONTO   SYDNEY   NEW DELHI

Adams Media
An Imprint of Simon & Schuster, Inc.
100 Technology Center Drive
Stoughton, Massachusetts 02072

First Adams Media hardcover edition May 2022

ADAMS MEDIA and colophon are trademarks of Simon & Schuster.

For information about special discounts for bulk purchases, please contact Simon & Schuster Special Sales at 1-866-506-1949 or business@simonandschuster.com.

The Simon & Schuster Speakers Bureau can bring authors to your live event. For more information or to book an event contact the Simon & Schuster Speakers Bureau at 1-866-248-3049 or visit our website at www.simonspeakers.com.

Interior design by Colleen Cunningham
Interior images © 123RF/morys, jeksonjs, dmstudio;
Getty Images/Siripak Pason
Map by Alaya Howard

Manufactured in China

10 9 8 7 6 5 4 3 2 1

ISBN 978-1-5072-1809-9

Dedication

For you.
For me.
For the Parks.
And for Jon, who explored them all with me.

CONTENTS

INTRODUCTION

Would you like to:

▶ Touch 220-million-year-old trees petrified into colorful kaleidoscopes of crystal?
▶ See 1,000-pound bears fishing in rivers and foraging in meadows?
▶ Wander through red rock wonderlands of soaring arches and natural formations?

You can see all this and more in America's national parks.

Our national parks are enjoying a renaissance—beckoning people of all ages and backgrounds, and with varying levels of skill and physical fitness who dream of visiting the places that have mesmerized millions. Whatever your dreams entail, with sixty-three national parks in thirty states and two US territories, picking which one to visit might be the hardest part!

To start, you'll need to plan. To go, you'll need to be equipped. And to store it in your memory bank, you'll want to cement your experiences in writing. That's where *The National Parks Journal* comes in! This book will be your companion as you voyage into America's cherished public lands. Inside you'll find pre-trip planning advice, packing ideas, and workbook sections designed to help you record your experiences.

Advance planning is vital when visiting the parks, and that's where you'll want to start in this journal. Where to go and where to stay are essentials, as are ideas for what to do when you get there and how you plan to get around. You'll also need packing tips like terrain-specific outdoor gear and advice on necessities like food and hydration so you can be better prepared and have what you need when you need it.

Once you're in the parks, it'll be time to capture some of that magic. Recording pages are part guided and part blank slate, with space to take notes and log memorable moments during your time in the great outdoors. Mark the pages up as you desire—this is your personalized handbook for all of your future national park voyages!

Whether you are looking for a day-trip adventure or an immersive week(s)- or month(s)-long stay, this book has almost all aspects of your trip covered. Think of this journal as your personal guide for your next great national parks journey. Whatever your inclination, adventure awaits!

HOW TO USE THIS BOOK

One of the beautiful things about the US national parks is that they were created specifically for the enjoyment of all people—in the beginning, now, and in the future. This journal is designed with that same philosophy in mind: to help you with preplanning, help you craft tailored adventures and experiences while in the parks, and encourage you to document your findings to file into your memory and to share with your loved ones and other park-goers.

Because there are so many wonderful ways to enjoy the parks—to lose yourself in a peaceful natural setting, witness magnificent landscapes, or push your body with physical activity—there cannot be a one-size-fits-all approach to planning an itinerary. With that in mind, this journal is not going to provide everything you will need to consider for your individualized journey. For example, if you are road-tripping in a van, RV, or travel trailer and planning an extended stay, you will have different needs than those who are zipping in for a day trip or passing through on a scenic drive. If you are exerting yourself on a big adventure, you will want to make sure to bring food that packs light and also has important nutritional value: carbs, proteins, and fats (yes, the parks are one place where extra calories work to your advantage). If you are a photographer, you'll want a gear bag with weather protection to keep your favorite lenses clean, whereas if you're a long-distance hiker setting out on the Appalachian Trail, extra pairs of socks and additional foot protection are going to be your new best friends.

The planning pages will help you consider the basics, such as where to stay, when to go, and what to do when you get there, and will also delve deeper into forward-prep that will aid in determinations such as whether you want to physically train prior to your adventure (so that you can hit that one epic trail a little bit harder).

Packing pages offer ideas of what to bring so that you are outfitted with the basics for a trip into the outdoors. The packing lists aren't all inclusive, as terrain and climate considerations vary greatly from one park to the next. For example, if you find yourself on a sprawling glacier without crampons or microspikes, on a washboard road without a spare tire, or on a rocky riverway without trekking poles in hand—you might find yourself in a bit of trouble.

The recording pages are a finishing touch—a snapshot of your time in the parks—where you can reflect on what you saw, capture moments you'll never want to forget, and note lessons learned that can help improve future experiences when you travel in the national parks or elsewhere in the future.

Each park adventure necessitates a good amount of additional research on your part as it relates to your specific plans... think of this as a reminder to look into additional details as a complement to the advice you will find throughout this journal.

· PART 1 ·

Getting to Know the US National Parks

A cross the US national parks, cast bronze plaques memorialize the contributions of the first director of the National Park Service, Stephen Mather, with these words: *He laid the foundation of the National Park Service, defining and establishing the policies under which its areas shall be developed and conserved, unimpaired for future generations. There will never come an end to the good he has done.*

The early dreams and promise of preserving the immeasurable value of America's treasured landscapes for future generations has come full circle, with a new generation of national park lovers enjoying the parks for themselves, then carrying on the tradition of sharing the public lands with their children and grandchildren, with the hope that they will do the same.

Parks stretch from Alaska to the US Virgin Islands, from Maine to American Samoa. They dot the landscape everywhere in between to form a collective ecosystem that tells a natural and cultural history of the United States. The National Park Service manages sixty-three flagship national parks, as well as national monuments, battlefields, historic sites, lakeshores and seashores; wild and scenic rivers and riverways; and scenic trails—and these are just a sample of twenty designations that comprise protected areas in all fifty states, the District of Columbia, and four US territories.

In this part, you will learn about the history of our national parks as well as the myriad types of areas that have earned this designation. You'll also find information about planning a trip to one of the sites, and get some tips on what you ought to be aware of before heading off to explore the vast wonders in America's public lands.

Understanding the Complexities of the National Park System

There are more than four hundred national parks (what writer and historian Wallace Stegner cited as "the best idea we ever had") in the United States spanning more than 85 million acres with unique designations, and it all began in 1872 when Yellowstone was established as the first national park. How did we get from an early concept of preserving a small group of unique places to a vast portfolio visited by hundreds of millions year after year? We can be certain that it wasn't just one thing, but rather that it took more than one hundred years of collective effort, exploration, and thorough documentation. This chapter will help you to discover more about the formation of the National Park Service, specific designations within the National Park System, and insider tips that will help you prepare for your trip and explore more responsibly.

A Brief History of the National Parks

When the US National Park Service was formed in 1916, there had been no effort like it before. Its construct would go on to serve as a global blueprint of how to shape comprehensive conservation efforts on a large scale, propelling ecotourism while safeguarding precious features that serve as a source of pride in countries all over the world.

That success hinges on the early efforts of several notable figures, including Scottish immigrant and naturalist John Muir (sometimes referred to as the "Father of the National Parks"); President Theodore Roosevelt (also known as "The Conservationist President"), who, after traveling with Muir through Yosemite, would go on to establish five national parks during his time in office; and President Woodrow Wilson, who established the National Park Service, appointing Stephen Mather as the first director.

Mather was a passionate adventurer and successful businessman who used his professional acumen to shape policy and earn greater support among lawmakers, while employing his know-how in branding and marketing to appeal to the curious masses. His imprint is felt throughout the parks today in grand entrance gates, ornate bridges, and historical visitor centers and park lodges constructed in National Park Service rustic–style (or "Parkitecture" as it's sometimes called)—an approach to architecture developed early on with the goal of creating harmony between the natural environment and new facilities built for staff and visitors.

Long before these men, Native Americans, Western settlers, explorers, and seafarers charted the unknown without modern-day tools like accurate maps that we have the benefit of using today. Those early trailblazers paved the way for later expeditions in mostly unmapped areas of the American West, which were storied at length in the private journals of US presidents, naturalists, scientists, and explorers, as well as famed authors, artists, and photographers who captured what they saw in prose, paintings, and verse. Like theirs, this journal can become a lasting way to capture your own park experiences.

A Breakdown of National Park Designations

Spanning 8 million acres, there are sixty-three national parks in the United States and in two US territories, and 423 park sites in all fifty states and four US territories. Designations are generally granted to places that hold natural, cultural, scenic, and scientific values and are largely classified by the level of federal legislation that brought them into the National Park System, along with agreements formed with state and local entities. Understanding the nuances can be confusing, so here is a basic breakdown:

▶ **National parks** can only be established by presidential proclamation or by acts of Congress. They generally encompass large expanses that contain a variety of land-, water-, and ecological-based attributes that could not be sustained without greater protection.

▶ **National monuments** protect at least one significant historical site or resource (such as Mount Rushmore in South Dakota), but may lack environmental diversity in immediately surrounding areas.

▶ **National preserves**, existing within national park boundaries in Alaska, Colorado, and West Virginia, conserve resources that allow for activities that subsistence communities rely on to retain rights that sustain their way of life, such as mineral extraction, hunting, and fishing.

▶ **National scenic trails** encompass interconnected scenic and recreational footpaths that carry historical significance. Some notable examples include the Appalachian, Pacific Crest, and Continental Divide Trails—the largest thru-hikes in the US.

▶ **National wild and scenic rivers and riverways** protect free-flowing waterways that exist in their purest state (those that have not been interfered with by human-made obstructions), while also providing recreational opportunities on self-propelled watercraft.

▶ **National rivers** preserve free-flowing waterways and have at least one unique natural or cultural aspect, and/or provide recreational value. The Buffalo National River in Arkansas, flowing unobstructed for 135 miles, was the first to receive this designation.

▶ **National seashores and lakeshores** are two separate designations protecting freshwater and saltwater shorelines and offshore islands, and allow for recreational use. They can be found coast-to-coast in places like Assateague Island in Maryland/Virginia and Point Reyes in northern California.

▶ **National memorials** preserve areas where notable events occurred and/or commemorate people who shaped the nation's history. Notable examples include the Vietnam Veterans Memorial in Washington, DC, and Pearl Harbor on the island of Oahu in Hawaii. These sites are sometimes called *Sites of Remembrance*.

▶ **National battlefields, battlefield parks, battlefield sites, and military parks** cover four separate designations protecting areas that honor America's military history—sites where notable battles were fought in the United States. Twenty-five battle sites are preserved to commemorate nation-shaping conflicts, ranging from attacks on Native Americans to events of the Civil War.

▶ **National historical parks, historic sites, and international historic sites** are three separate designations that commemorate human history—running the gamut from indigenous sites to areas that have shaped modern-day America. Examples include the Knife River Indian Villages in North Dakota and the Harriet Tubman Underground Railroad in Maryland. There is only one international historic site in the system: Saint Croix Island in Maine (bordering New Brunswick in Canada), the first permanent French settlement in North America.

▶ **National parkways** are designated scenic roadways that weave through national parklands. There are four in the National Park System, including the Blue Ridge Parkway (Virginia/North Carolina), the George Washington Memorial Parkway (Virginia/Washington, DC/Maryland), the John D. Rockefeller Jr. Memorial Parkway connecting Grand Teton and Yellowstone National Parks, and the Natchez Trace Parkway (Mississippi/Tennessee).

▶ **National reserves** are areas that protect important plants and wildlife and are generally managed in partnership with local and state authorities. Ebey's Landing in Washington state and the City of Rocks in Idaho are the only two in the system.

▶ **National recreation areas** preserve land and water features for conservation coinciding with recreational use, such as hiking and wildlife viewing; boating and fishing; and horseback riding. Some examples include the Santa Monica Mountains in California, known for great hiking and endangered mountain lion populations, and Lake Chelan in Washington, a hot spot for camping and summer watersports.

Planning Advice for Your Journey

This book is all about helping you plan, pack for, and record your national park experiences. Think of this section as a precursor to the upcoming checklist and write-in pages—it will spur your planning mindset with useful tips for preparation, smart tools and hacks used by seasoned park travelers, and a few important notes on how to explore responsibly.

Research In Advance
Many of the great park experiences have already been explored by others, and you can use their knowledge, pointers, and missteps to your advantage! Conducting location-based web searches before your trip can turn up unexpectedly cool and lesser-known sights, top-notch regional outfitters, and adventures you haven't yet considered but are suddenly dying to try. Searching "national park images" on the web is also a smart idea, as it can provide a glimpse of how others are capturing iconic scenes and also possibly inspire ideas on how you can put your own stamp on your park photography.

Make Reservations
Whether it be for popular hiking trails, campgrounds, or sometimes even viewpoints—reservations made in advance can help improve your experience by minimizing wait times while making life easier for Park Service staff managing these areas.

Take Pictures
Snapping a quick shot of trailheads, parking spots, and other reference points of where you are traveling can help you find your way back if you get turned around.

Also, remember: safety first, pictures second. Whether you are determined to photograph wildlife or a beautiful landscape, it's important to remember that animals will not pose, and sprawling views are often seen from areas that can be treacherous—such as near rivers, sheer drops, or on scrambling trails. You might need to wait for the right conditions to capture your magic shot. Patience and careful steps are key.

Plan to Explore Lesser-Known Areas

Hitting off-the-beaten-trail landmarks, trail systems, and road routes can offer a taste of the uncommon and unfamiliar, while minimizing impact at heavily trafficked locations. Ask rangers in the visitor centers for advice on lesser-known places they love to explore—they can reveal hidden gems that are typically every bit as awesome as more touristy areas. As you share these experiences, you'll see how excited others become learning about places they've perhaps never heard of.

Leave Behind a Trip Plan

Outline your route and itinerary, planned dates of departure and return, scheduled activities, recognizable equipment you'll tote (e.g., tent color, car make and model, and so on), and any specific medical needs you might have. Leave one copy at home with a loved one and one copy on the dash or in the glove box of your vehicle. This information is invaluable to rescue teams in an emergency situation.

Useful Tools and Advice to Help You Explore

With more than a century of experience hosting outdoor enthusiasts from around the world, the National Park Service knows a thing or two about providing guidance to park visitors. The following resources are free (with the exception of the annual pass) and will open your mind to all there is to see in the national parks.

▶ **Access the visitor centers.** Safety and ease start in the NPS visitor centers! Rangers and staff know of closures, current local weather systems, and countless other bits of information that can make all the difference once you step foot into the parks.

▶ **Get to know the rangers.** They are there to help and are ready to provide insider tips, give you intel on recent wildlife sightings, and guide you along complex trail systems. They have great stories to tell too!

▶ **Join ranger-led activities.** National Park ranger–led outings abound in the parks! They are fun for kids and adults alike, are usually relatively short in duration, and allow you to ask questions while exploring and learning about some of the most frequented areas. You can learn more about them in the park visitor centers.

▶ **Try out audio- and auto-touring guides.** Many of the national parks provide self-guided audio- and auto-tours, which are a great way of learning more about what you are seeing in areas that have multiple points of interest. Inquire about these in park visitor centers.

▶ **Check out the NPS webcams.** Want to know if wildflowers are at peak bloom? Or if bald eagle eaglets are about to hatch? Want to find out what marine life is up to in sawgrass marshes or beneath the surface of the sea? There is a full list of webcams on the National Park Service official website! Simply go to NPS .gov and search "webcams" to find which are presently most active. Webcams can sometimes help steer your journey, and can also inspire you from the comfort of your home or on your mobile device while you're on the road.

▶ **Pick up park brochures at the entrance gates.** National park brochures and park newspapers given at points-of-entry offer current information, including special events, trail maps, and insight into what each particular park is best known for.

▶ **Use the NPS mobile app.** The NPS has a world-class mobile app covering the full National Park System portfolio. From the palm of your hand you can tap in to general information, get a lay of the land with interactive maps, save favorite places, make must-see lists, and uncover plenty more that can enhance your national park adventures. Download before you go! The NPS app is free and available for iOS and Android devices.

▶ **Consider buying an annual pass.** If you plan to visit multiple parks within the space of one year, an annual America the Beautiful national parks pass will save you money. You can purchase it for $80. Individual vehicle entries can cost up to $35 per day—which can add up quickly—making the annual pass entirely worthwhile. Military passes (free) and senior passes ($80 lifetime/$20 annual) are also available.

Explore Responsibly!

Responsible visitation is a must to ensure that we are preserving America's most special places for future generations to enjoy, the way that they were preserved for us. Respecting the natural environment, other visitors, and shared surroundings, and minding safety rules administered by the National Park Service, are just a few examples of what it means to explore responsibly.

▶ **Stay on-trail.** Veering off established trails is prohibited unless exploring areas designated for backcountry use, and for good reason: The national parks are active scientific test beds where important conservation is always at work!

▶ **Be patient.** There will be traffic jams leading into popular parks. There will be "bear jams" when cars stop unexpectedly for wildlife sightings. There may be lines in the NPS visitor centers while seeking information or permits, and then more lines on trails as hikers work their way through congested areas. It is important for the safety of all that patience is exercised while in the parks.

▶ **Be a responsible pet owner.** Dream of exploring the parks with your dog in tow? Learn the rules of your chosen park before you go. Leashed dogs are often allowed in campgrounds and on some trails, though factors like wildlife, delicate landscapes, and the safety of other visitors may prevent them from joining you in many areas.

▶ **Be careful around wildlife.** Animals are *wild*, and that's why they are so exciting to see! Do not feed them and never approach. Think of yourself as a guest in their environment, and never underestimate their unpredictability.

▶ **Leave no trace.** *Take only memories and pictures, leave only footprints.*—one of the parks' monikers that pretty much says it all! Search "Leave No Trace Seven Principles" on NPS.gov to learn more about outdoor ethics.

The US National Parks

Of the 423 park sites, the sixty-three that follow are those that have an official "national park" designation. (Some parks are in more than one state.)

Alaska

☐ Denali National Park and Preserve   DATE:

☐ Gates of the Arctic National Park and Preserve   DATE:

☐ Glacier Bay National Park and Preserve   DATE:

☐ Katmai National Park and Preserve   DATE:

☐ Kenai Fjords National Park   DATE:

☐ Kobuk Valley National Park   DATE:

☐ Lake Clark National Park and Preserve   DATE:

☐ Wrangell-St. Elias National Park and Preserve   DATE:

American Samoa

☐ National Park of American Samoa   DATE:

Arizona

☐ Grand Canyon National Park   DATE:

☐ Petrified Forest National Park   DATE:

☐ Saguaro National Park   DATE:

Arkansas

❏ Hot Springs National Park   DATE:

California

❏ Channel Islands National Park   DATE:

❏ Death Valley National Park   DATE:

❏ Joshua Tree National Park   DATE:

❏ Kings Canyon National Park   DATE:

❏ Lassen Volcanic National Park   DATE:

❏ Pinnacles National Park   DATE:

❏ Redwood National and State Parks   DATE:

❏ Sequoia National Park   DATE:

❏ Yosemite National Park   DATE:

Colorado

❏ Black Canyon of the Gunnison National Park   DATE:

❏ Great Sand Dunes National Park and Preserve   DATE:

❏ Mesa Verde National Park   DATE:

❏ Rocky Mountain National Park   DATE:

Florida

❏ Biscayne National Park   DATE:

❏ Dry Tortugas National Park   DATE:

❏ Everglades National Park   DATE:

Hawaii

❏ Haleakalā National Park DATE:

❏ Hawai'i Volcanoes National Park DATE:

Idaho

❏ Yellowstone National Park DATE:

Indiana

❏ Indiana Dunes National Park DATE:

Kentucky

❏ Mammoth Cave National Park DATE:

Maine

❏ Acadia National Park DATE:

Michigan

❏ Isle Royale National Park DATE:

Minnesota

❏ Voyageurs National Park DATE:

Missouri

❏ Gateway Arch National Park DATE:

Montana

❏ Glacier National Park DATE:

❏ Yellowstone National Park DATE:

Nevada

❏ Death Valley National Park   DATE:

❏ Great Basin National Park   DATE:

New Mexico

❏ Carlsbad Caverns National Park   DATE:

❏ White Sands National Park   DATE:

North Carolina

❏ Great Smoky Mountains National Park   DATE:

North Dakota

❏ Theodore Roosevelt National Park   DATE:

Ohio

❏ Cuyahoga Valley National Park   DATE:

Oregon

❏ Crater Lake National Park   DATE:

South Carolina

❏ Congaree National Park   DATE:

South Dakota

❏ Badlands National Park   DATE:

❏ Wind Cave National Park   DATE:

Tennessee

❏ Great Smoky Mountains National Park   DATE:

Texas

❑ Big Bend National Park   DATE:

❑ Guadalupe Mountains National Park   DATE:

US Virgin Islands

❑ Virgin Islands National Park   DATE:

Utah

❑ Arches National Park   DATE:

❑ Bryce Canyon National Park   DATE:

❑ Canyonlands National Park   DATE:

❑ Capitol Reef National Park   DATE:

❑ Zion National Park   DATE:

Virginia

❑ Shenandoah National Park   DATE:

Washington

❑ Mount Rainier National Park   DATE:

❑ North Cascades National Park   DATE:

❑ Olympic National Park   DATE:

West Virginia

❑ New River Gorge National Park and Preserve   DATE:

Wyoming

❑ Grand Teton National Park   DATE:

❑ Yellowstone National Park   DATE:

MAP
OF THE US NATIONAL PARKS

1. Acadia National Park
2. Arches National Park
3. Badlands National Park
4. Big Bend National Park
5. Biscayne National Park
6. Black Canyon of the Gunnison National Park
7. Bryce Canyon National Park
8. Canyonlands National Park
9. Capitol Reef National Park
10. Carlsbad Caverns National Park
11. Channel Islands National Park
12. Congaree National Park
13. Crater Lake National Park
14. Cuyahoga Valley National Park
15. Death Valley National Park
16. Denali National Park and Preserve
17. Dry Tortugas National Park
18. Everglades National Park
19. Gates of the Arctic National Park and Preserve
20. Gateway Arch National Park
21. Glacier Bay National Park and Preserve
22. Glacier National Park
23. Grand Canyon National Park
24. Grand Teton National Park
25. Great Basin National Park
26. Great Sand Dunes National Park and Preserve
27. Great Smoky Mountains National Park

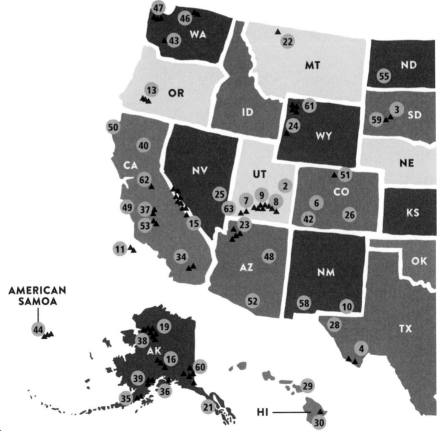

28. Guadalupe Mountains National Park
29. Haleakalā National Park
30. Hawai'i Volcanoes National Park
31. Hot Springs National Park
32. Indiana Dunes National Park
33. Isle Royale National Park
34. Joshua Tree National Park
35. Katmai National Park and Preserve
36. Kenai Fjords National Park
37. Kings Canyon National Park
38. Kobuk Valley National Park
39. Lake Clark National Park and Preserve
40. Lassen Volcanic National Park
41. Mammoth Cave National Park
42. Mesa Verde National Park
43. Mount Rainier National Park
44. National Park of American Samoa
45. New River Gorge National Park and
    Preserve

46. North Cascades National Park
47. Olympic National Park
48. Petrified Forest National Park
49. Pinnacles National Park
50. Redwood National and State Parks
51. Rocky Mountain National Park
52. Saguaro National Park
53. Sequoia National Park
54. Shenandoah National Park
55. Theodore Roosevelt National Park
56. Virgin Islands National Park
57. Voyageurs National Park
58. White Sands National Park
59. Wind Cave National Park
60. Wrangell-St. Elias National Park
    and Preserve
61. Yellowstone National Park
62. Yosemite National Park
63. Zion National Park

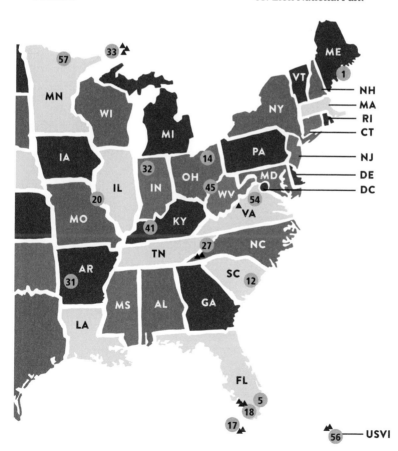

· PART 2 ·

Enhancing Your National Park Experience

The following pages will help steer your preparation so that you can make the most out of your time in America's national parks. You'll find pages dedicated to planning, packing, and recording your experiences, with plenty of space where you can outline the individual needs of your trip.

Pages in checklist/write-in format allow you to evaluate the basics of organizing an outdoor adventure and may encourage untapped ideas. As you navigate the thinking process, you might realize that in addition to your initial adventure goals, you may also want to try out a new sport or outing led by National Park Service staff or outfitters in towns neighboring the parks. Perhaps you're on a no-plan plan, but then decide that you might benefit from the knowledge of guides who know specificities of individual regions, terrain, and wildlife. The included sections are meant to initiate this kind of brainstorming.

Once you have the basics of your visit outlined in the planning pages, it's time to consider what you'll want to pack (and what you might need to purchase) to better equip yourself for your trip. Beyond the basics of appropriate clothing, footwear, and outdoor gear, you'll find ideas ranging from illumination tools like headlamps to miscellaneous items like trash bags (so that you "leave no trace" while in the parks).

With your packing plans underway, don't forget to utilize the additional notes sections where you can jot down questions spurred from what you find (or don't find) in the preceding pages.

Finally, the recording pages are designated to help you capture all you are seeing and enjoying most while spending time in the parks. You'll also find an arrowhead rating on these pages—inspired by the arrowhead insignia of the National Park Service—where you can rate your experiences.

PLAN YOUR TRIP!

Park name: ....

State/territory: ....   Temperature range: ....

Planned dates: ....   Altitude range: ....

Time zone: ....   Latitude/longitude: ....

COMMITMENT LEVEL

- 6 — Full throttle, all-in adventure time!
- 5 — Bring on a big challenge!
- 4 — Many trails, sites, & adventures planned!
- 3 — Rolling where the wind blows me!
- 2 — Tons to do without breaking a big sweat!
- 1 — Easy-going, leisurely days...

SEASON OF VISIT

- ☐ Spring
- ☐ Summer
- ☐ Autumn
- ☐ Winter

TOURING/SUPPORT

- ☐ Self-guided
- ☐ Privately guided
- ☐ Chartered trip
- ☐ Group trip
- ☐ Volunteering
- ☐ Ranger-led tours
- ☐ Instructional classes
- ☐ Special events
- ....
- ....
- ....
- ....
- ....

PARK TRANSPORT

- ☐ Car
- ☐ Bus
- ☐ RV/travel trailer
- ☐ Boat
- ☐ Float plane/bush plane
- ☐ Helicopter
- ☐ Tour bus
- ☐ All-terrain vehicle
- ☐ ....

PARK ITEMS TO PICK UP

- ☐ NPS annual pass
- ☐ NPS parks passport
- ☐ Pins, patches, & stickers
- ☐ Hiking stick medallions
- ☐ NPS maps & literature
- ☐ ....
- ☐ ....
- ☐ ....

RESOURCES/CONTACTS

- ☐ NPS visitor center(s):
  ....
- ☐ Wilderness permit(s):
  ....
- ☐ Tour company:
  ....
- ☐ Local guide(s):
  ....
- ☐ Local gear outfitter(s):
  ....
- ☐ Emergency services:
  ....
- ☐ Miscellaneous contact:
  ....
- ☐ Miscellaneous contact:
  ....

MAIN ACCOMMODATIONS

- ☐ NPS lodge
- ☐ Hotel
- ☐ RV/travel trailer
- ☐ Tent camping
- ☐ Backcountry camping
- ☐ Staying with friends
- ☐ Houseboat
- ☐ Cruise ship
- ☐ Van/car
- ☐ ....
- ☐ ....

AMENITIES

- [ ] Campgrounds
  - [ ] Standard
  - [ ] RV
  - [ ] Primitive
  - [ ] Day use only
  - [ ] Group
- [ ] Plumbed bathrooms
- [ ] Showers
- [ ] Park store
- [ ] Wi-Fi
- [ ] NPS amphitheater
- [ ] Pet-friendly
- [ ] ------------------------------
- [ ] ------------------------------

IN-TOW

- [ ] Spouse/partner
- [ ] Children
- [ ] Pets
- [ ] Friends
- [ ] Extended family
- [ ] Boatloads of gear!
- [ ] ------------------------------
- [ ] ------------------------------

ADVANCED PLANNING

- [ ] Physical training?

- [ ] Seasonal aspects?

- [ ] Obtained permits?

- [ ] Purchased gear?

FINAL SAFETY CHECKS

- [ ] Left your trip plan with an emergency contact back home?
- [ ] Reviewed basic emergency aid procedures?
- [ ] Additional forms/permits needed?
- [ ] Checked on closures/mandates that might affect your travel?
- [ ] ------------------------------
- [ ] ------------------------------
- [ ] ------------------------------

MAIN GOALS

- [ ] Solitude
- [ ] Active adventure
- [ ] Creative pursuits
- [ ] Learning
- [ ] Endurance training
- [ ] Gathering loved ones
- [ ] Seeing new things!
- [ ] ------------------------------
- [ ] ------------------------------
- [ ] ------------------------------

IMMERSIVE EXPERIENCES

- [ ] Cultural/historical
- [ ] Volunteering
- [ ] Park programs
- [ ] Junior Ranger program
- [ ] NPS-guided night walks
- [ ] School/youth trips
- [ ] Teacher/educator programs
- [ ] Professional development
- [ ] ------------------------------
- [ ] ------------------------------
- [ ] ------------------------------

ADVENTURE GOALS

- [ ] Hiking big trails
- [ ] Easy day hikes
- [ ] Cycling/mountain biking/fat biking
- [ ] Kayaking/canoeing/SUP
- [ ] Trail running
- [ ] Rafting
- [ ] Swimming
- [ ] Backpacking
- [ ] Wildlife viewing
- [ ] Scenic drives
- [ ] Fishing/angling
- [ ] Mountaineering
- [ ] Climbing/bouldering
- [ ] Photography
- [ ] Birdwatching
- [ ] Stargazing
- [ ] Cultural immersion
- [ ] Endurance training
- [ ] Picnicking
- [ ] ------------------------------

PHOTOGRAPHY PLANS

- [ ] Wildlife
- [ ] Birds
- [ ] Landscapes
- [ ] Night skies
- [ ] People
- [ ] Cultural artifacts
- [ ] Macro/abstract
- [ ] Family pictures
- [ ] Selfies
- [ ] ------------------------------

ADDITIONAL NOTES

PACK FOR YOUR TRIP!

Park name: ....

- ☐ Premade first aid kit
- ☐ Wildlife/insect protection
- ☐ Medications
- ☐ ....
- ☐ ....
- ☐ Supplements
- ☐ ....
- ☐ ....
- ☐ Eyeglasses/contacts
- ☐ Sun/wind/snow protection (eyes/skin/face)
- ☐ Facial tissues
- ☐ Bug spray
- ☐ Antibacterial wipes
- ☐ ....
- ☐ ....

ELECTRONICS

- ☐ Camera
  - ☐ Tripod
  - ☐ Lenses/lens cloths
  - ☐ Memory cards
  - ☐ Batteries & charger
- ☐ Weather protection
- ☐ External charging device
- ☐ Phone & charging cord
- ☐ Mobile Wi-Fi device
- ☐ Electronic tablet
- ☐ Satellite phone
- ☐ Personal locater beacon
- ☐ ....

CLOTHING/SHOES

- ☐ Insulated jacket
- ☐ Rain jacket/pants
- ☐ Thermal layers
- ☐ Wicked/quick-dry clothing
- ☐ Loose-fitting shirts
- ☐ Loose-fitting pants
- ☐ Hiking pants/shorts
- ☐ Short-sleeved/sleeveless shirts
- ☐ Full winter gear
- ☐ ....
- ☐ ....
- ☐ ....
- ☐ Leisurewear
- ☐ Beachwear
- ☐ Hiking shoes
- ☐ Athletic shoes
- ☐ Water shoes
- ☐ Sandals/flip-flops
- ☐ Neck gaiter
- ☐ Sun hat/cap
- ☐ Stocking cap
- ☐ Socks + extra pair
- ☐ Undergarments
- ☐ Gloves/mittens
- ☐ ....
- ☐ ....
- ☐ ....
- ☐ ....
- ☐ ....
- ☐ ....
- ☐ ....
- ☐ ....

OUTDOOR GEAR

- ☐ Hiking poles
- ☐ Tent
- ☐ Sleeping bag
- ☐ Sleeping pad
- ☐ Pillow
- ☐ Shade tent
- ☐ Emergency space blanket
- ☐ Tarp
- ☐ Daypack
- ☐ Headlamp(s)
- ☐ Lantern(s)
- ☐ Water filter & iodine tablets
- ☐ Large refillable water jug
- ☐ Portable stove
- ☐ Hot beverage thermos
- ☐ Nylon hammock
- ☐ Throw blanket
- ☐ Reusable dishes/cutlery
- ☐ Hand warmers
- ☐ ....
- ☐ ....
- ☐ ....
- ☐ ....
- ☐ ....
- ☐ ....
- ☐ ....
- ☐ ....
- ☐ ....
- ☐ ....

FOOD & DRINK

- [ ] Water
- [ ] Refillable water bottle
- [ ] Energy drinks with electrolytes
- [ ] Protein-packed snacks
- [ ] Salty, easy-to-digest snacks
- [ ] Dehydrated food
- [ ] No-cook food items
- [ ] ....
- [ ] ....
- [ ] ....
- [ ] ....
- [ ] ....
- [ ] ....
- [ ] ....
- [ ] ....
- [ ] ....
- [ ] ....
- [ ] ....
- [ ] ....
- [ ] ....
- [ ] ....
- [ ] ....

PARK-SPECIFIC

- [ ] *The National Parks Journal*!
- [ ] Permits
- [ ] Guidebooks
- [ ] Park map
- [ ] ....
- [ ] ....
- [ ] ....
- [ ] ....
- [ ] ....
- [ ] ....

MISCELLANEOUS

- [ ] Duct tape
- [ ] Multipurpose tool
- [ ] Knife
- [ ] Scissors
- [ ] Can opener
- [ ] Matches/lighter/firestarter
- [ ] Hatchet
- [ ] Whistle
- [ ] Bandana
- [ ] Quick-dry towels
- [ ] Waterproof bags
- [ ] Ziplock bags
- [ ] Trash bags
- [ ] Paper towels
- [ ] Bear can
- [ ] Binoculars
- [ ] Deck of cards/games
- [ ] Driver's license, registration, insurance, etc.
- [ ] Spare tire/jack
- [ ] Wiper blades
- [ ] Small amount of cash
- [ ] ....
- [ ] ....
- [ ] ....
- [ ] ....
- [ ] ....
- [ ] ....
- [ ] ....
- [ ] ....
- [ ] ....
- [ ] ....
- [ ] ....
- [ ] ....
- [ ] ....

PERSONALIZED LIST

- [ ] ....
- [ ] ....
- [ ] ....
- [ ] ....
- [ ] ....
- [ ] ....
- [ ] ....
- [ ] ....
- [ ] ....

TO BUY

- [ ] ....
- [ ] ....
- [ ] ....
- [ ] ....
- [ ] ....
- [ ] ....
- [ ] ....
- [ ] ....
- [ ] ....

ADDITIONAL NOTES

RECORD YOUR TRIP!

Park name: ....

State/territory: ....

Dates visited: ....

Nearby sites visited: ....

ARROWHEAD RATING!

🔹 5 — Epic & life-changing experience

🔹 4 — Want to learn everything about this park!

🔹 3 — See why this place is so special

🔹 2 — Happy I went and had some good times

🔹 1 — Once and done!

FAVORITE CAMPSITE OR LODGING: ....

....

PEAK EXPERIENCE: ....

....

FAVORITE ADVENTURE: ....

....

FAVORITE LOCATION: ....

....

FAVORITE PHOTO: ....

....

BEST WILDLIFE SIGHTING: ....

....

FUN THING(S) I LEARNED ABOUT THE PARK: ....

....

INTERESTING PEOPLE MET ALONG MY JOURNEY: ....

....

VALUABLE RESOURCE(S) DISCOVERED ALONG THE WAY: ....

....

FOOD I COULDN'T LIVE WITHOUT: ....

....

THE BIGGEST CHALLENGE I FACED: ....

....

I WAS MOST PREPARED WHEN: ....

....

WISH I KNEW BEFORE I WENT: ....

....

WISH I WOULD HAVE BROUGHT: ....

....

MOST USEFUL PIECE OF GEAR: ....

....

MOST VALUABLE TOOL: ....

....

MOST USEFUL PIECE OF ADVICE: ....

....

TIPS FOR OTHER TRAVELERS: ....

....

ADDITIONAL NOTES: ....

....

....

....

PLAN YOUR TRIP!

Park name: ....

State/territory: ....   Temperature range: ....

Planned dates: ....   Altitude range: ....

Time zone: ....   Latitude/longitude: ....

COMMITMENT LEVEL

- 6 — Full throttle, all-in adventure time!
- 5 — Bring on a big challenge!
- 4 — Many trails, sites, & adventures planned!
- 3 — Rolling where the wind blows me!
- 2 — Tons to do without breaking a big sweat!
- 1 — Easy-going, leisurely days...

SEASON OF VISIT

- ☐ Spring
- ☐ Summer
- ☐ Autumn
- ☐ Winter

TOURING/SUPPORT

- ☐ Self-guided
- ☐ Privately guided
- ☐ Chartered trip
- ☐ Group trip
- ☐ Volunteering
- ☐ Ranger-led tours
- ☐ Instructional classes
- ☐ Special events
- ☐ ----------------------------
- ☐ ----------------------------
- ☐ ----------------------------
- ☐ ----------------------------
- ☐ ----------------------------

PARK TRANSPORT

- ☐ Car
- ☐ Bus
- ☐ RV/travel trailer
- ☐ Boat
- ☐ Float plane/bush plane
- ☐ Helicopter
- ☐ Tour bus
- ☐ All-terrain vehicle
- ☐ ----------------------------

PARK ITEMS TO PICK UP

- ☐ NPS annual pass
- ☐ NPS parks passport
- ☐ Pins, patches, & stickers
- ☐ Hiking stick medallions
- ☐ NPS maps & literature
- ☐ ----------------------------
- ☐ ----------------------------
- ☐ ----------------------------

RESOURCES/CONTACTS

- ☐ NPS visitor center(s):
- ☐ Wilderness permit(s):
- ☐ Tour company:
- ☐ Local guide(s):
- ☐ Local gear outfitter(s):
- ☐ Emergency services:
- ☐ Miscellaneous contact:
- ☐ Miscellaneous contact:

MAIN ACCOMMODATIONS

- ☐ NPS lodge
- ☐ Hotel
- ☐ RV/travel trailer
- ☐ Tent camping
- ☐ Backcountry camping
- ☐ Staying with friends
- ☐ Houseboat
- ☐ Cruise ship
- ☐ Van/car
- ☐ ----------------------------
- ☐ ----------------------------

AMENITIES

- [ ] Campgrounds
  - [ ] Standard
  - [ ] RV
  - [ ] Primitive
  - [ ] Day use only
  - [ ] Group
- [ ] Plumbed bathrooms
- [ ] Showers
- [ ] Park store
- [ ] Wi-Fi
- [ ] NPS amphitheater
- [ ] Pet-friendly
- [ ] ....
- [ ] ....

IN-TOW

- [ ] Spouse/partner
- [ ] Children
- [ ] Pets
- [ ] Friends
- [ ] Extended family
- [ ] Boatloads of gear!
- [ ] ....
- [ ] ....

ADVANCED PLANNING

- [ ] Physical training?

  ....
  ....
- [ ] Seasonal aspects?

  ....
  ....
- [ ] Obtained permits?

  ....
  ....
- [ ] Purchased gear?

  ....
  ....
  ....

FINAL SAFETY CHECKS

- [ ] Left your trip plan with an emergency contact back home?
- [ ] Reviewed basic emergency aid procedures?
- [ ] Additional forms/permits needed?
- [ ] Checked on closures/mandates that might affect your travel?
- [ ] ....
- [ ] ....
- [ ] ....

MAIN GOALS

- [ ] Solitude
- [ ] Active adventure
- [ ] Creative pursuits
- [ ] Learning
- [ ] Endurance training
- [ ] Gathering loved ones
- [ ] Seeing new things!
- [ ] ....
- [ ] ....
- [ ] ....

IMMERSIVE EXPERIENCES

- [ ] Cultural/historical
- [ ] Volunteering
- [ ] Park programs
- [ ] Junior Ranger program
- [ ] NPS-guided night walks
- [ ] School/youth trips
- [ ] Teacher/educator programs
- [ ] Professional development
- [ ] ....
- [ ] ....
- [ ] ....

ADVENTURE GOALS

- [ ] Hiking big trails
- [ ] Easy day hikes
- [ ] Cycling/mountain biking/fat biking
- [ ] Kayaking/canoeing/SUP
- [ ] Trail running
- [ ] Rafting
- [ ] Swimming
- [ ] Backpacking
- [ ] Wildlife viewing
- [ ] Scenic drives
- [ ] Fishing/angling
- [ ] Mountaineering
- [ ] Climbing/bouldering
- [ ] Photography
- [ ] Birdwatching
- [ ] Stargazing
- [ ] Cultural immersion
- [ ] Endurance training
- [ ] Picnicking
- [ ] ....

PHOTOGRAPHY PLANS

- [ ] Wildlife
- [ ] Birds
- [ ] Landscapes
- [ ] Night skies
- [ ] People
- [ ] Cultural artifacts
- [ ] Macro/abstract
- [ ] Family pictures
- [ ] Selfies
- [ ] ....

ADDITIONAL NOTES

....
....
....
....

PACK FOR YOUR TRIP!

Park name: ....

HEALTH & PERSONAL ITEMS

- [ ] Premade first aid kit
- [ ] Wildlife/insect protection
- [ ] Medications
- [ ] ....
- [ ] ....
- [ ] Supplements
- [ ] ....
- [ ] ....
- [ ] Eyeglasses/contacts
- [ ] Sun/wind/snow protection (eyes/skin/face)
- [ ] Facial tissues
- [ ] Bug spray
- [ ] Antibacterial wipes
- [ ] ....
- [ ] ....

ELECTRONICS

- [ ] Camera
  - [ ] Tripod
  - [ ] Lenses/lens cloths
  - [ ] Memory cards
  - [ ] Batteries & charger
- [ ] Weather protection
- [ ] External charging device
- [ ] Phone & charging cord
- [ ] Mobile Wi-Fi device
- [ ] Electronic tablet
- [ ] Satellite phone
- [ ] Personal locater beacon
- [ ] ....

CLOTHING/SHOES

- [ ] Insulated jacket
- [ ] Rain jacket/pants
- [ ] Thermal layers
- [ ] Wicked/quick-dry clothing
- [ ] Loose-fitting shirts
- [ ] Loose-fitting pants
- [ ] Hiking pants/shorts
- [ ] Short-sleeved/sleeveless shirts
- [ ] Full winter gear
- [ ] ....
- [ ] ....
- [ ] ....
- [ ] Leisurewear
- [ ] Beachwear
- [ ] Hiking shoes
- [ ] Athletic shoes
- [ ] Water shoes
- [ ] Sandals/flip-flops
- [ ] Neck gaiter
- [ ] Sun hat/cap
- [ ] Stocking cap
- [ ] Socks + extra pair
- [ ] Undergarments
- [ ] Gloves/mittens
- [ ] ....
- [ ] ....
- [ ] ....
- [ ] ....
- [ ] ....
- [ ] ....
- [ ] ....

OUTDOOR GEAR

- [ ] Hiking poles
- [ ] Tent
- [ ] Sleeping bag
- [ ] Sleeping pad
- [ ] Pillow
- [ ] Shade tent
- [ ] Emergency space blanket
- [ ] Tarp
- [ ] Daypack
- [ ] Headlamp(s)
- [ ] Lantern(s)
- [ ] Water filter & iodine tablets
- [ ] Large refillable water jug
- [ ] Portable stove
- [ ] Hot beverage thermos
- [ ] Nylon hammock
- [ ] Throw blanket
- [ ] Reusable dishes/cutlery
- [ ] Hand warmers
- [ ] ....
- [ ] ....
- [ ] ....
- [ ] ....
- [ ] ....
- [ ] ....
- [ ] ....
- [ ] ....
- [ ] ....
- [ ] ....
- [ ] ....

FOOD & DRINK

- [ ] Water
- [ ] Refillable water bottle
- [ ] Energy drinks with electrolytes
- [ ] Protein-packed snacks
- [ ] Salty, easy-to-digest snacks
- [ ] Dehydrated food
- [ ] No-cook food items
- [ ] ....
- [ ] ....
- [ ] ....
- [ ] ....
- [ ] ....
- [ ] ....
- [ ] ....
- [ ] ....
- [ ] ....
- [ ] ....
- [ ] ....
- [ ] ....
- [ ] ....
- [ ] ....

PARK-SPECIFIC

- [ ] *The National Parks Journal*!
- [ ] Permits
- [ ] Guidebooks
- [ ] Park map
- [ ] ....
- [ ] ....
- [ ] ....
- [ ] ....
- [ ] ....
- [ ] ....
- [ ] ....

MISCELLANEOUS

- [ ] Duct tape
- [ ] Multipurpose tool
- [ ] Knife
- [ ] Scissors
- [ ] Can opener
- [ ] Matches/lighter/ firestarter
- [ ] Hatchet
- [ ] Whistle
- [ ] Bandana
- [ ] Quick-dry towels
- [ ] Waterproof bags
- [ ] Ziplock bags
- [ ] Trash bags
- [ ] Paper towels
- [ ] Bear can
- [ ] Binoculars
- [ ] Deck of cards/games
- [ ] Driver's license, registration, insurance, etc.
- [ ] Spare tire/jack
- [ ] Wiper blades
- [ ] Small amount of cash
- [ ] ....
- [ ] ....
- [ ] ....
- [ ] ....
- [ ] ....
- [ ] ....
- [ ] ....
- [ ] ....
- [ ] ....
- [ ] ....
- [ ] ....
- [ ] ....
- [ ] ....
- [ ] ....
- [ ] ....
- [ ] ....

PERSONALIZED LIST

- [ ] ....
- [ ] ....
- [ ] ....
- [ ] ....
- [ ] ....
- [ ] ....
- [ ] ....
- [ ] ....
- [ ] ....

TO BUY

- [ ] ....
- [ ] ....
- [ ] ....
- [ ] ....
- [ ] ....
- [ ] ....
- [ ] ....
- [ ] ....
- [ ] ....
- [ ] ....

ADDITIONAL NOTES

RECORD YOUR TRIP!

Park name: ....

State/territory: ....

Dates visited: ....

Nearby sites visited: ....

ARROWHEAD RATING!

5 — Epic & life-changing experience

4 — Want to learn everything about this park!

3 — See why this place is so special

2 — Happy I went and had some good times

1 — Once and done!

FAVORITE CAMPSITE OR LODGING: ....

....

PEAK EXPERIENCE: ....

....

FAVORITE ADVENTURE: ....

....

FAVORITE LOCATION: ....

....

FAVORITE PHOTO: ....

....

BEST WILDLIFE SIGHTING: ....

....

FUN THING(S) I LEARNED ABOUT THE PARK: ....

....

INTERESTING PEOPLE MET ALONG MY JOURNEY:

VALUABLE RESOURCE(S) DISCOVERED ALONG THE WAY:

FOOD I COULDN'T LIVE WITHOUT:

THE BIGGEST CHALLENGE I FACED:

I WAS MOST PREPARED WHEN:

WISH I KNEW BEFORE I WENT:

WISH I WOULD HAVE BROUGHT:

MOST USEFUL PIECE OF GEAR:

MOST VALUABLE TOOL:

MOST USEFUL PIECE OF ADVICE:

TIPS FOR OTHER TRAVELERS:

ADDITIONAL NOTES:

PLAN YOUR TRIP!

Park name: ....

State/territory: ....   Temperature range: ....

Planned dates: ....   Altitude range: ....

Time zone: ....   Latitude/longitude: ....

COMMITMENT LEVEL

- 6 — Full throttle, all-in adventure time!
- 5 — Bring on a big challenge!
- 4 — Many trails, sites, & adventures planned!
- 3 — Rolling where the wind blows me!
- 2 — Tons to do without breaking a big sweat!
- 1 — Easy-going, leisurely days...

SEASON OF VISIT

- ☐ Spring
- ☐ Summer
- ☐ Autumn
- ☐ Winter

TOURING/SUPPORT

- ☐ Self-guided
- ☐ Privately guided
- ☐ Chartered trip
- ☐ Group trip
- ☐ Volunteering
- ☐ Ranger-led tours
- ☐ Instructional classes
- ☐ Special events
- ....
- ....
- ....
- ....
- ....

PARK TRANSPORT

- ☐ Car
- ☐ Bus
- ☐ RV/travel trailer
- ☐ Boat
- ☐ Float plane/bush plane
- ☐ Helicopter
- ☐ Tour bus
- ☐ All-terrain vehicle
- ☐ ....

PARK ITEMS TO PICK UP

- ☐ NPS annual pass
- ☐ NPS parks passport
- ☐ Pins, patches, & stickers
- ☐ Hiking stick medallions
- ☐ NPS maps & literature
- ☐ ....
- ☐ ....
- ☐ ....

RESOURCES/CONTACTS

- ☐ NPS visitor center(s):
  ....
- ☐ Wilderness permit(s):
  ....
- ☐ Tour company:
  ....
- ☐ Local guide(s):
  ....
- ☐ Local gear outfitter(s):
  ....
- ☐ Emergency services:
  ....
- ☐ Miscellaneous contact:
  ....
- ☐ Miscellaneous contact:
  ....

MAIN ACCOMMODATIONS

- ☐ NPS lodge
- ☐ Hotel
- ☐ RV/travel trailer
- ☐ Tent camping
- ☐ Backcountry camping
- ☐ Staying with friends
- ☐ Houseboat
- ☐ Cruise ship
- ☐ Van/car
- ☐ ....

AMENITIES

- [ ] Campgrounds
  - [ ] Standard
  - [ ] RV
  - [ ] Primitive
  - [ ] Day use only
  - [ ] Group
- [ ] Plumbed bathrooms
- [ ] Showers
- [ ] Park store
- [ ] Wi-Fi
- [ ] NPS amphitheater
- [ ] Pet-friendly
- [ ] --------------------------
- [ ] --------------------------

IN-TOW

- [ ] Spouse/partner
- [ ] Children
- [ ] Pets
- [ ] Friends
- [ ] Extended family
- [ ] Boatloads of gear!
- [ ] --------------------------
- [ ] --------------------------

ADVANCED PLANNING

- [ ] Physical training?

- [ ] Seasonal aspects?

- [ ] Obtained permits?

- [ ] Purchased gear?

FINAL SAFETY CHECKS

- [ ] Left your trip plan with an emergency contact back home?
- [ ] Reviewed basic emergency aid procedures?
- [ ] Additional forms/permits needed?
- [ ] Checked on closures/mandates that might affect your travel?
- [ ] --------------------------
- [ ] --------------------------
- [ ] --------------------------

MAIN GOALS

- [ ] Solitude
- [ ] Active adventure
- [ ] Creative pursuits
- [ ] Learning
- [ ] Endurance training
- [ ] Gathering loved ones
- [ ] Seeing new things!
- [ ] --------------------------
- [ ] --------------------------
- [ ] --------------------------

IMMERSIVE EXPERIENCES

- [ ] Cultural/historical
- [ ] Volunteering
- [ ] Park programs
- [ ] Junior Ranger program
- [ ] NPS-guided night walks
- [ ] School/youth trips
- [ ] Teacher/educator programs
- [ ] Professional development
- [ ] --------------------------
- [ ] --------------------------
- [ ] --------------------------

ADVENTURE GOALS

- [ ] Hiking big trails
- [ ] Easy day hikes
- [ ] Cycling/mountain biking/fat biking
- [ ] Kayaking/canoeing/SUP
- [ ] Trail running
- [ ] Rafting
- [ ] Swimming
- [ ] Backpacking
- [ ] Wildlife viewing
- [ ] Scenic drives
- [ ] Fishing/angling
- [ ] Mountaineering
- [ ] Climbing/bouldering
- [ ] Photography
- [ ] Birdwatching
- [ ] Stargazing
- [ ] Cultural immersion
- [ ] Endurance training
- [ ] Picnicking
- [ ] --------------------------

PHOTOGRAPHY PLANS

- [ ] Wildlife
- [ ] Birds
- [ ] Landscapes
- [ ] Night skies
- [ ] People
- [ ] Cultural artifacts
- [ ] Macro/abstract
- [ ] Family pictures
- [ ] Selfies
- [ ] --------------------------

ADDITIONAL NOTES

PACK FOR YOUR TRIP!

Park name: ....

HEALTH & PERSONAL ITEMS

- [ ] Premade first aid kit
- [ ] Wildlife/insect protection
- [ ] Medications
- [ ] ....
- [ ] ....
- [ ] Supplements
- [ ] ....
- [ ] Eyeglasses/contacts
- [ ] Sun/wind/snow protection (eyes/skin/face)
- [ ] Facial tissues
- [ ] Bug spray
- [ ] Antibacterial wipes
- [ ] ....
- [ ] ....

ELECTRONICS

- [ ] Camera
  - [ ] Tripod
  - [ ] Lenses/lens cloths
  - [ ] Memory cards
  - [ ] Batteries & charger
- [ ] Weather protection
- [ ] External charging device
- [ ] Phone & charging cord
- [ ] Mobile Wi-Fi device
- [ ] Electronic tablet
- [ ] Satellite phone
- [ ] Personal locater beacon
- [ ] ....

CLOTHING/SHOES

- [ ] Insulated jacket
- [ ] Rain jacket/pants
- [ ] Thermal layers
- [ ] Wicked/quick-dry clothing
- [ ] Loose-fitting shirts
- [ ] Loose-fitting pants
- [ ] Hiking pants/shorts
- [ ] Short-sleeved/sleeveless shirts
- [ ] Full winter gear
- [ ] ....
- [ ] ....
- [ ] ....
- [ ] Leisurewear
- [ ] Beachwear
- [ ] Hiking shoes
- [ ] Athletic shoes
- [ ] Water shoes
- [ ] Sandals/flip-flops
- [ ] Neck gaiter
- [ ] Sun hat/cap
- [ ] Stocking cap
- [ ] Socks + extra pair
- [ ] Undergarments
- [ ] Gloves/mittens
- [ ] ....
- [ ] ....
- [ ] ....
- [ ] ....
- [ ] ....
- [ ] ....
- [ ] ....

OUTDOOR GEAR

- [ ] Hiking poles
- [ ] Tent
- [ ] Sleeping bag
- [ ] Sleeping pad
- [ ] Pillow
- [ ] Shade tent
- [ ] Emergency space blanket
- [ ] Tarp
- [ ] Daypack
- [ ] Headlamp(s)
- [ ] Lantern(s)
- [ ] Water filter & iodine tablets
- [ ] Large refillable water jug
- [ ] Portable stove
- [ ] Hot beverage thermos
- [ ] Nylon hammock
- [ ] Throw blanket
- [ ] Reusable dishes/cutlery
- [ ] Hand warmers
- [ ] ....
- [ ] ....
- [ ] ....
- [ ] ....
- [ ] ....
- [ ] ....
- [ ] ....
- [ ] ....
- [ ] ....
- [ ] ....
- [ ] ....

FOOD & DRINK

- [ ] Water
- [ ] Refillable water bottle
- [ ] Energy drinks with electrolytes
- [ ] Protein-packed snacks
- [ ] Salty, easy-to-digest snacks
- [ ] Dehydrated food
- [ ] No-cook food items
- [ ] ....
- [ ] ....
- [ ] ....
- [ ] ....
- [ ] ....
- [ ] ....
- [ ] ....
- [ ] ....
- [ ] ....
- [ ] ....
- [ ] ....
- [ ] ....
- [ ] ....
- [ ] ....
- [ ] ....
- [ ] ....
- [ ] ....

PARK-SPECIFIC

- [ ] *The National Parks Journal*!
- [ ] Permits
- [ ] Guidebooks
- [ ] Park map
- [ ] ....
- [ ] ....
- [ ] ....
- [ ] ....
- [ ] ....
- [ ] ....
- [ ] ....

MISCELLANEOUS

- [ ] Duct tape
- [ ] Multipurpose tool
- [ ] Knife
- [ ] Scissors
- [ ] Can opener
- [ ] Matches/lighter/firestarter
- [ ] Hatchet
- [ ] Whistle
- [ ] Bandana
- [ ] Quick-dry towels
- [ ] Waterproof bags
- [ ] Ziplock bags
- [ ] Trash bags
- [ ] Paper towels
- [ ] Bear can
- [ ] Binoculars
- [ ] Deck of cards/games
- [ ] Driver's license, registration, insurance, etc.
- [ ] Spare tire/jack
- [ ] Wiper blades
- [ ] Small amount of cash
- [ ] ....
- [ ] ....
- [ ] ....
- [ ] ....
- [ ] ....
- [ ] ....
- [ ] ....
- [ ] ....
- [ ] ....
- [ ] ....
- [ ] ....
- [ ] ....
- [ ] ....
- [ ] ....

PERSONALIZED LIST

- [ ] ....
- [ ] ....
- [ ] ....
- [ ] ....
- [ ] ....
- [ ] ....
- [ ] ....
- [ ] ....
- [ ] ....
- [ ] ....
- [ ] ....

TO BUY

- [ ] ....
- [ ] ....
- [ ] ....
- [ ] ....
- [ ] ....
- [ ] ....
- [ ] ....
- [ ] ....
- [ ] ....
- [ ] ....

ADDITIONAL NOTES

RECORD YOUR TRIP!

Park name: ....

State/territory: ....

Dates visited: ....

Nearby sites visited: ....

ARROWHEAD RATING!

- 5 — Epic & life-changing experience
- 4 — Want to learn everything about this park!
- 3 — See why this place is so special
- 2 — Happy I went and had some good times
- 1 — Once and done!

FAVORITE CAMPSITE OR LODGING: ....

PEAK EXPERIENCE: ....

FAVORITE ADVENTURE: ....

FAVORITE LOCATION: ....

FAVORITE PHOTO: ....

BEST WILDLIFE SIGHTING: ....

FUN THING(S) I LEARNED ABOUT THE PARK: ....

INTERESTING PEOPLE MET ALONG MY JOURNEY: ....

....

VALUABLE RESOURCE(S) DISCOVERED ALONG THE WAY: ....

....

FOOD I COULDN'T LIVE WITHOUT: ....

....

THE BIGGEST CHALLENGE I FACED: ....

....

I WAS MOST PREPARED WHEN: ....

....

WISH I KNEW BEFORE I WENT: ....

....

WISH I WOULD HAVE BROUGHT: ....

....

MOST USEFUL PIECE OF GEAR: ....

....

MOST VALUABLE TOOL: ....

....

MOST USEFUL PIECE OF ADVICE: ....

....

TIPS FOR OTHER TRAVELERS: ....

....

ADDITIONAL NOTES: ....

....

....

....

....

PLAN YOUR TRIP!

Park name: ....

State/territory: ....   Temperature range: ....

Planned dates: ....   Altitude range: ....

Time zone: ....   Latitude/longitude: ....

COMMITMENT LEVEL

- 6 — Full throttle, all-in adventure time!
- 5 — Bring on a big challenge!
- 4 — Many trails, sites, & adventures planned!
- 3 — Rolling where the wind blows me!
- 2 — Tons to do without breaking a big sweat!
- 1 — Easy-going, leisurely days...

SEASON OF VISIT

- ☐ Spring
- ☐ Summer
- ☐ Autumn
- ☐ Winter

TOURING/SUPPORT

- ☐ Self-guided
- ☐ Privately guided
- ☐ Chartered trip
- ☐ Group trip
- ☐ Volunteering
- ☐ Ranger-led tours
- ☐ Instructional classes
- ☐ Special events
- ☐ ....
- ☐ ....
- ☐ ....
- ☐ ....
- ☐ ....

PARK TRANSPORT

- ☐ Car
- ☐ Bus
- ☐ RV/travel trailer
- ☐ Boat
- ☐ Float plane/bush plane
- ☐ Helicopter
- ☐ Tour bus
- ☐ All-terrain vehicle
- ☐ ....

PARK ITEMS TO PICK UP

- ☐ NPS annual pass
- ☐ NPS parks passport
- ☐ Pins, patches, & stickers
- ☐ Hiking stick medallions
- ☐ NPS maps & literature
- ☐ ....
- ☐ ....
- ☐ ....

RESOURCES/CONTACTS

- ☐ NPS visitor center(s):
  ....
- ☐ Wilderness permit(s):
  ....
- ☐ Tour company:
  ....
- ☐ Local guide(s):
  ....
- ☐ Local gear outfitter(s):
  ....
- ☐ Emergency services:
  ....
- ☐ Miscellaneous contact:
  ....
- ☐ Miscellaneous contact:
  ....

MAIN ACCOMMODATIONS

- ☐ NPS lodge
- ☐ Hotel
- ☐ RV/travel trailer
- ☐ Tent camping
- ☐ Backcountry camping
- ☐ Staying with friends
- ☐ Houseboat
- ☐ Cruise ship
- ☐ Van/car
- ☐ ....
- ☐ ....

AMENITIES

- [ ] Campgrounds
  - [ ] Standard
  - [ ] RV
  - [ ] Primitive
  - [ ] Day use only
  - [ ] Group
- [ ] Plumbed bathrooms
- [ ] Showers
- [ ] Park store
- [ ] Wi-Fi
- [ ] NPS amphitheater
- [ ] Pet-friendly
- [ ] ....
- [ ] ....

IN-TOW

- [ ] Spouse/partner
- [ ] Children
- [ ] Pets
- [ ] Friends
- [ ] Extended family
- [ ] Boatloads of gear!
- [ ] ....
- [ ] ....

ADVANCED PLANNING

- [ ] Physical training?

....

....

- [ ] Seasonal aspects?

....

....

- [ ] Obtained permits?

....

....

- [ ] Purchased gear?

....

....

....

FINAL SAFETY CHECKS

- [ ] Left your trip plan with an emergency contact back home?
- [ ] Reviewed basic emergency aid procedures?
- [ ] Additional forms/permits needed?
- [ ] Checked on closures/mandates that might affect your travel?
- [ ] ....
- [ ] ....
- [ ] ....

MAIN GOALS

- [ ] Solitude
- [ ] Active adventure
- [ ] Creative pursuits
- [ ] Learning
- [ ] Endurance training
- [ ] Gathering loved ones
- [ ] Seeing new things!
- [ ] ....
- [ ] ....
- [ ] ....

IMMERSIVE EXPERIENCES

- [ ] Cultural/historical
- [ ] Volunteering
- [ ] Park programs
- [ ] Junior Ranger program
- [ ] NPS-guided night walks
- [ ] School/youth trips
- [ ] Teacher/educator programs
- [ ] Professional development
- [ ] ....
- [ ] ....
- [ ] ....

ADVENTURE GOALS

- [ ] Hiking big trails
- [ ] Easy day hikes
- [ ] Cycling/mountain biking/fat biking
- [ ] Kayaking/canoeing/SUP
- [ ] Trail running
- [ ] Rafting
- [ ] Swimming
- [ ] Backpacking
- [ ] Wildlife viewing
- [ ] Scenic drives
- [ ] Fishing/angling
- [ ] Mountaineering
- [ ] Climbing/bouldering
- [ ] Photography
- [ ] Birdwatching
- [ ] Stargazing
- [ ] Cultural immersion
- [ ] Endurance training
- [ ] Picnicking
- [ ] ....

PHOTOGRAPHY PLANS

- [ ] Wildlife
- [ ] Birds
- [ ] Landscapes
- [ ] Night skies
- [ ] People
- [ ] Cultural artifacts
- [ ] Macro/abstract
- [ ] Family pictures
- [ ] Selfies
- [ ] ....

ADDITIONAL NOTES

....

....

....

....

PACK FOR YOUR TRIP!

Park name: ....

HEALTH & PERSONAL ITEMS

- [ ] Premade first aid kit
- [ ] Wildlife/insect protection
- [ ] Medications
- [ ] ....
- [ ] ....
- [ ] Supplements
- [ ] ....
- [ ] ....
- [ ] Eyeglasses/contacts
- [ ] Sun/wind/snow protection (eyes/skin/face)
- [ ] Facial tissues
- [ ] Bug spray
- [ ] Antibacterial wipes
- [ ] ....
- [ ] ....

ELECTRONICS

- [ ] Camera
  - [ ] Tripod
  - [ ] Lenses/lens cloths
  - [ ] Memory cards
  - [ ] Batteries & charger
- [ ] Weather protection
- [ ] External charging device
- [ ] Phone & charging cord
- [ ] Mobile Wi-Fi device
- [ ] Electronic tablet
- [ ] Satellite phone
- [ ] Personal locater beacon
- [ ] ....

CLOTHING/SHOES

- [ ] Insulated jacket
- [ ] Rain jacket/pants
- [ ] Thermal layers
- [ ] Wicked/quick-dry clothing
- [ ] Loose-fitting shirts
- [ ] Loose-fitting pants
- [ ] Hiking pants/shorts
- [ ] Short-sleeved/sleeveless shirts
- [ ] Full winter gear
- [ ] ....
- [ ] ....
- [ ] ....
- [ ] Leisurewear
- [ ] Beachwear
- [ ] Hiking shoes
- [ ] Athletic shoes
- [ ] Water shoes
- [ ] Sandals/flip-flops
- [ ] Neck gaiter
- [ ] Sun hat/cap
- [ ] Stocking cap
- [ ] Socks + extra pair
- [ ] Undergarments
- [ ] Gloves/mittens
- [ ] ....
- [ ] ....
- [ ] ....
- [ ] ....
- [ ] ....
- [ ] ....
- [ ] ....
- [ ] ....

OUTDOOR GEAR

- [ ] Hiking poles
- [ ] Tent
- [ ] Sleeping bag
- [ ] Sleeping pad
- [ ] Pillow
- [ ] Shade tent
- [ ] Emergency space blanket
- [ ] Tarp
- [ ] Daypack
- [ ] Headlamp(s)
- [ ] Lantern(s)
- [ ] Water filter & iodine tablets
- [ ] Large refillable water jug
- [ ] Portable stove
- [ ] Hot beverage thermos
- [ ] Nylon hammock
- [ ] Throw blanket
- [ ] Reusable dishes/cutlery
- [ ] Hand warmers
- [ ] ....
- [ ] ....
- [ ] ....
- [ ] ....
- [ ] ....
- [ ] ....
- [ ] ....
- [ ] ....
- [ ] ....
- [ ] ....
- [ ] ....

FOOD & DRINK

- [ ] Water
- [ ] Refillable water bottle
- [ ] Energy drinks with electrolytes
- [ ] Protein-packed snacks
- [ ] Salty, easy-to-digest snacks
- [ ] Dehydrated food
- [ ] No-cook food items
- [ ] ....
- [ ] ....
- [ ] ....
- [ ] ....
- [ ] ....
- [ ] ....
- [ ] ....
- [ ] ....
- [ ] ....
- [ ] ....
- [ ] ....
- [ ] ....
- [ ] ....
- [ ] ....
- [ ] ....

PARK-SPECIFIC

- [ ] *The National Parks Journal*!
- [ ] Permits
- [ ] Guidebooks
- [ ] Park map
- [ ] ....
- [ ] ....
- [ ] ....
- [ ] ....
- [ ] ....
- [ ] ....

MISCELLANEOUS

- [ ] Duct tape
- [ ] Multipurpose tool
- [ ] Knife
- [ ] Scissors
- [ ] Can opener
- [ ] Matches/lighter/firestarter
- [ ] Hatchet
- [ ] Whistle
- [ ] Bandana
- [ ] Quick-dry towels
- [ ] Waterproof bags
- [ ] Ziplock bags
- [ ] Trash bags
- [ ] Paper towels
- [ ] Bear can
- [ ] Binoculars
- [ ] Deck of cards/games
- [ ] Driver's license, registration, insurance, etc.
- [ ] Spare tire/jack
- [ ] Wiper blades
- [ ] Small amount of cash
- [ ] ....
- [ ] ....
- [ ] ....
- [ ] ....
- [ ] ....
- [ ] ....
- [ ] ....
- [ ] ....
- [ ] ....
- [ ] ....
- [ ] ....
- [ ] ....
- [ ] ....
- [ ] ....

PERSONALIZED LIST

- [ ] ....
- [ ] ....
- [ ] ....
- [ ] ....
- [ ] ....
- [ ] ....
- [ ] ....
- [ ] ....
- [ ] ....
- [ ] ....

TO BUY

- [ ] ....
- [ ] ....
- [ ] ....
- [ ] ....
- [ ] ....
- [ ] ....
- [ ] ....
- [ ] ....
- [ ] ....
- [ ] ....

ADDITIONAL NOTES

RECORD YOUR TRIP!

Park name: ....

State/territory: ....

Dates visited: ....

Nearby sites visited: ....

5 — Epic & life-changing experience
4 — Want to learn everything about this park!
3 — See why this place is so special
2 — Happy I went and had some good times
1 — Once and done!

FAVORITE CAMPSITE OR LODGING: ....

....

PEAK EXPERIENCE: ....

....

FAVORITE ADVENTURE: ....

....

FAVORITE LOCATION: ....

....

FAVORITE PHOTO: ....

....

BEST WILDLIFE SIGHTING: ....

....

FUN THING(S) I LEARNED ABOUT THE PARK: ....

....

INTERESTING PEOPLE MET ALONG MY JOURNEY: ....

....

VALUABLE RESOURCE(S) DISCOVERED ALONG THE WAY: ....

....

FOOD I COULDN'T LIVE WITHOUT: ....

....

THE BIGGEST CHALLENGE I FACED: ....

....

I WAS MOST PREPARED WHEN: ....

....

WISH I KNEW BEFORE I WENT: ....

....

WISH I WOULD HAVE BROUGHT: ....

....

MOST USEFUL PIECE OF GEAR: ....

....

MOST VALUABLE TOOL: ....

....

MOST USEFUL PIECE OF ADVICE: ....

....

TIPS FOR OTHER TRAVELERS: ....

....

ADDITIONAL NOTES: ....

....

....

....

....

PLAN YOUR TRIP!

Park name: ....

State/territory: ....   Temperature range: ....

Planned dates: ....   Altitude range: ....

Time zone: ....   Latitude/longitude: ....

COMMITMENT LEVEL

6 — Full throttle, all-in adventure time!

5 — Bring on a big challenge!

4 — Many trails, sites, & adventures planned!

3 — Rolling where the wind blows me!

2 — Tons to do without breaking a big sweat!

1 — Easy-going, leisurely days...

SEASON OF VISIT

☐ Spring
☐ Summer
☐ Autumn
☐ Winter

TOURING/SUPPORT

☐ Self-guided
☐ Privately guided
☐ Chartered trip
☐ Group trip
☐ Volunteering
☐ Ranger-led tours
☐ Instructional classes
☐ Special events
....
....
....
....
....

PARK TRANSPORT

☐ Car
☐ Bus
☐ RV/travel trailer
☐ Boat
☐ Float plane/bush plane
☐ Helicopter
☐ Tour bus
☐ All-terrain vehicle
☐ ....

PARK ITEMS TO PICK UP

☐ NPS annual pass
☐ NPS parks passport
☐ Pins, patches, & stickers
☐ Hiking stick medallions
☐ NPS maps & literature
☐ ....
☐ ....
☐ ....

RESOURCES/CONTACTS

☐ NPS visitor center(s):
....
☐ Wilderness permit(s):
....
☐ Tour company:
....
☐ Local guide(s):
....
☐ Local gear outfitter(s):
....
☐ Emergency services:
....
☐ Miscellaneous contact:
....
☐ Miscellaneous contact:
....

MAIN ACCOMMODATIONS

☐ NPS lodge
☐ Hotel
☐ RV/travel trailer
☐ Tent camping
☐ Backcountry camping
☐ Staying with friends
☐ Houseboat
☐ Cruise ship
☐ Van/car
☐ ....
☐ ....

AMENITIES

- [ ] Campgrounds
  - [ ] Standard
  - [ ] RV
  - [ ] Primitive
  - [ ] Day use only
  - [ ] Group
- [ ] Plumbed bathrooms
- [ ] Showers
- [ ] Park store
- [ ] Wi-Fi
- [ ] NPS amphitheater
- [ ] Pet-friendly
- [ ] ....
- [ ] ....

IN-TOW

- [ ] Spouse/partner
- [ ] Children
- [ ] Pets
- [ ] Friends
- [ ] Extended family
- [ ] Boatloads of gear!
- [ ] ....
- [ ] ....

ADVANCED PLANNING

- [ ] Physical training?

  ....
  ....
- [ ] Seasonal aspects?

  ....
  ....
- [ ] Obtained permits?

  ....
  ....
- [ ] Purchased gear?

  ....
  ....
  ....

FINAL SAFETY CHECKS

- [ ] Left your trip plan with an emergency contact back home?
- [ ] Reviewed basic emergency aid procedures?
- [ ] Additional forms/permits needed?
- [ ] Checked on closures/mandates that might affect your travel?
- [ ] ....
- [ ] ....
- [ ] ....

MAIN GOALS

- [ ] Solitude
- [ ] Active adventure
- [ ] Creative pursuits
- [ ] Learning
- [ ] Endurance training
- [ ] Gathering loved ones
- [ ] Seeing new things!
- [ ] ....
- [ ] ....
- [ ] ....

IMMERSIVE EXPERIENCES

- [ ] Cultural/historical
- [ ] Volunteering
- [ ] Park programs
- [ ] Junior Ranger program
- [ ] NPS-guided night walks
- [ ] School/youth trips
- [ ] Teacher/educator programs
- [ ] Professional development
- [ ] ....
- [ ] ....
- [ ] ....

ADVENTURE GOALS

- [ ] Hiking big trails
- [ ] Easy day hikes
- [ ] Cycling/mountain biking/fat biking
- [ ] Kayaking/canoeing/SUP
- [ ] Trail running
- [ ] Rafting
- [ ] Swimming
- [ ] Backpacking
- [ ] Wildlife viewing
- [ ] Scenic drives
- [ ] Fishing/angling
- [ ] Mountaineering
- [ ] Climbing/bouldering
- [ ] Photography
- [ ] Birdwatching
- [ ] Stargazing
- [ ] Cultural immersion
- [ ] Endurance training
- [ ] Picnicking
- [ ] ....

PHOTOGRAPHY PLANS

- [ ] Wildlife
- [ ] Birds
- [ ] Landscapes
- [ ] Night skies
- [ ] People
- [ ] Cultural artifacts
- [ ] Macro/abstract
- [ ] Family pictures
- [ ] Selfies
- [ ] ....

ADDITIONAL NOTES

....
....
....
....

PACK FOR YOUR TRIP!

Park name: ....

HEALTH & PERSONAL ITEMS

- [ ] Premade first aid kit
- [ ] Wildlife/insect protection
- [ ] Medications
- [ ] ....
- [ ] ....
- [ ] Supplements
- [ ] ....
- [ ] Eyeglasses/contacts
- [ ] Sun/wind/snow protection (eyes/skin/face)
- [ ] Facial tissues
- [ ] Bug spray
- [ ] Antibacterial wipes
- [ ] ....
- [ ] ....

ELECTRONICS

- [ ] Camera
  - [ ] Tripod
  - [ ] Lenses/lens cloths
  - [ ] Memory cards
  - [ ] Batteries & charger
- [ ] Weather protection
- [ ] External charging device
- [ ] Phone & charging cord
- [ ] Mobile Wi-Fi device
- [ ] Electronic tablet
- [ ] Satellite phone
- [ ] Personal locater beacon
- [ ] ....

CLOTHING/SHOES

- [ ] Insulated jacket
- [ ] Rain jacket/pants
- [ ] Thermal layers
- [ ] Wicked/quick-dry clothing
- [ ] Loose-fitting shirts
- [ ] Loose-fitting pants
- [ ] Hiking pants/shorts
- [ ] Short-sleeved/sleeveless shirts
- [ ] Full winter gear
- [ ] ....
- [ ] ....
- [ ] ....
- [ ] Leisurewear
- [ ] Beachwear
- [ ] Hiking shoes
- [ ] Athletic shoes
- [ ] Water shoes
- [ ] Sandals/flip-flops
- [ ] Neck gaiter
- [ ] Sun hat/cap
- [ ] Stocking cap
- [ ] Socks + extra pair
- [ ] Undergarments
- [ ] Gloves/mittens
- [ ] ....
- [ ] ....
- [ ] ....
- [ ] ....
- [ ] ....
- [ ] ....
- [ ] ....

OUTDOOR GEAR

- [ ] Hiking poles
- [ ] Tent
- [ ] Sleeping bag
- [ ] Sleeping pad
- [ ] Pillow
- [ ] Shade tent
- [ ] Emergency space blanket
- [ ] Tarp
- [ ] Daypack
- [ ] Headlamp(s)
- [ ] Lantern(s)
- [ ] Water filter & iodine tablets
- [ ] Large refillable water jug
- [ ] Portable stove
- [ ] Hot beverage thermos
- [ ] Nylon hammock
- [ ] Throw blanket
- [ ] Reusable dishes/cutlery
- [ ] Hand warmers
- [ ] ....
- [ ] ....
- [ ] ....
- [ ] ....
- [ ] ....
- [ ] ....
- [ ] ....
- [ ] ....
- [ ] ....
- [ ] ....

FOOD & DRINK

- [ ] Water
- [ ] Refillable water bottle
- [ ] Energy drinks with electrolytes
- [ ] Protein-packed snacks
- [ ] Salty, easy-to-digest snacks
- [ ] Dehydrated food
- [ ] No-cook food items
- [ ] ....
- [ ] ....
- [ ] ....
- [ ] ....
- [ ] ....
- [ ] ....
- [ ] ....
- [ ] ....
- [ ] ....
- [ ] ....
- [ ] ....
- [ ] ....
- [ ] ....
- [ ] ....
- [ ] ....

PARK-SPECIFIC

- [ ] *The National Parks Journal*!
- [ ] Permits
- [ ] Guidebooks
- [ ] Park map
- [ ] ....
- [ ] ....
- [ ] ....
- [ ] ....
- [ ] ....
- [ ] ....
- [ ] ....

MISCELLANEOUS

- [ ] Duct tape
- [ ] Multipurpose tool
- [ ] Knife
- [ ] Scissors
- [ ] Can opener
- [ ] Matches/lighter/firestarter
- [ ] Hatchet
- [ ] Whistle
- [ ] Bandana
- [ ] Quick-dry towels
- [ ] Waterproof bags
- [ ] Ziplock bags
- [ ] Trash bags
- [ ] Paper towels
- [ ] Bear can
- [ ] Binoculars
- [ ] Deck of cards/games
- [ ] Driver's license, registration, insurance, etc.
- [ ] Spare tire/jack
- [ ] Wiper blades
- [ ] Small amount of cash
- [ ] ....
- [ ] ....
- [ ] ....
- [ ] ....
- [ ] ....
- [ ] ....
- [ ] ....
- [ ] ....
- [ ] ....
- [ ] ....
- [ ] ....
- [ ] ....
- [ ] ....

PERSONALIZED LIST

- [ ] ....
- [ ] ....
- [ ] ....
- [ ] ....
- [ ] ....
- [ ] ....
- [ ] ....
- [ ] ....
- [ ] ....
- [ ] ....

TO BUY

- [ ] ....
- [ ] ....
- [ ] ....
- [ ] ....
- [ ] ....
- [ ] ....
- [ ] ....
- [ ] ....
- [ ] ....

ADDITIONAL NOTES

....
....
....
....
....
....
....
....
....
....
....
....
....
....

RECORD YOUR TRIP!

Park name: ....

State/territory: ....

Dates visited: ....

Nearby sites visited: ....

ARROWHEAD RATING!

5 — Epic & life-changing experience
4 — Want to learn everything about this park!
3 — See why this place is so special
2 — Happy I went and had some good times
1 — Once and done!

FAVORITE CAMPSITE OR LODGING: ....

PEAK EXPERIENCE: ....

FAVORITE ADVENTURE: ....

FAVORITE LOCATION: ....

FAVORITE PHOTO: ....

BEST WILDLIFE SIGHTING: ....

FUN THING(S) I LEARNED ABOUT THE PARK: ....

INTERESTING PEOPLE MET ALONG MY JOURNEY: ....

....

VALUABLE RESOURCE(S) DISCOVERED ALONG THE WAY: ....

....

FOOD I COULDN'T LIVE WITHOUT: ....

....

THE BIGGEST CHALLENGE I FACED: ....

....

I WAS MOST PREPARED WHEN: ....

....

WISH I KNEW BEFORE I WENT: ....

....

WISH I WOULD HAVE BROUGHT: ....

....

MOST USEFUL PIECE OF GEAR: ....

....

MOST VALUABLE TOOL: ....

....

MOST USEFUL PIECE OF ADVICE: ....

....

TIPS FOR OTHER TRAVELERS: ....

....

ADDITIONAL NOTES: ....

....

....

....

....

PLAN YOUR TRIP!

Park name: ....

State/territory: .... Temperature range: ....

Planned dates: .... Altitude range: ....

Time zone: .... Latitude/longitude: ....

COMMITMENT LEVEL

- 6 — Full throttle, all-in adventure time!
- 5 — Bring on a big challenge!
- 4 — Many trails, sites, & adventures planned!
- 3 — Rolling where the wind blows me!
- 2 — Tons to do without breaking a big sweat!
- 1 — Easy-going, leisurely days...

SEASON OF VISIT

- ☐ Spring
- ☐ Summer
- ☐ Autumn
- ☐ Winter

TOURING/SUPPORT

- ☐ Self-guided
- ☐ Privately guided
- ☐ Chartered trip
- ☐ Group trip
- ☐ Volunteering
- ☐ Ranger-led tours
- ☐ Instructional classes
- ☐ Special events
- ....
- ....
- ....
- ....
- ....

PARK TRANSPORT

- ☐ Car
- ☐ Bus
- ☐ RV/travel trailer
- ☐ Boat
- ☐ Float plane/bush plane
- ☐ Helicopter
- ☐ Tour bus
- ☐ All-terrain vehicle
- ☐ ....

PARK ITEMS TO PICK UP

- ☐ NPS annual pass
- ☐ NPS parks passport
- ☐ Pins, patches, & stickers
- ☐ Hiking stick medallions
- ☐ NPS maps & literature
- ☐ ....
- ☐ ....
- ☐ ....

RESOURCES/CONTACTS

- ☐ NPS visitor center(s):
  ....
- ☐ Wilderness permit(s):
  ....
- ☐ Tour company:
  ....
- ☐ Local guide(s):
  ....
- ☐ Local gear outfitter(s):
  ....
- ☐ Emergency services:
  ....
- ☐ Miscellaneous contact:
  ....
- ☐ Miscellaneous contact:
  ....

MAIN ACCOMMODATIONS

- ☐ NPS lodge
- ☐ Hotel
- ☐ RV/travel trailer
- ☐ Tent camping
- ☐ Backcountry camping
- ☐ Staying with friends
- ☐ Houseboat
- ☐ Cruise ship
- ☐ Van/car
- ☐ ....
- ☐ ....

AMENITIES

- [ ] Campgrounds
  - [ ] Standard
  - [ ] RV
  - [ ] Primitive
  - [ ] Day use only
  - [ ] Group
- [ ] Plumbed bathrooms
- [ ] Showers
- [ ] Park store
- [ ] Wi-Fi
- [ ] NPS amphitheater
- [ ] Pet-friendly
- [ ] ⋯⋯⋯⋯⋯⋯⋯
- [ ] ⋯⋯⋯⋯⋯⋯⋯

IN-TOW

- [ ] Spouse/partner
- [ ] Children
- [ ] Pets
- [ ] Friends
- [ ] Extended family
- [ ] Boatloads of gear!
- [ ] ⋯⋯⋯⋯⋯⋯⋯
- [ ] ⋯⋯⋯⋯⋯⋯⋯

ADVANCED PLANNING

- [ ] Physical training?

  ⋯⋯⋯⋯⋯⋯⋯
  ⋯⋯⋯⋯⋯⋯⋯
- [ ] Seasonal aspects?

  ⋯⋯⋯⋯⋯⋯⋯
  ⋯⋯⋯⋯⋯⋯⋯
- [ ] Obtained permits?

  ⋯⋯⋯⋯⋯⋯⋯
  ⋯⋯⋯⋯⋯⋯⋯
- [ ] Purchased gear?

  ⋯⋯⋯⋯⋯⋯⋯
  ⋯⋯⋯⋯⋯⋯⋯
  ⋯⋯⋯⋯⋯⋯⋯

FINAL SAFETY CHECKS

- [ ] Left your trip plan with an emergency contact back home?
- [ ] Reviewed basic emergency aid procedures?
- [ ] Additional forms/permits needed?
- [ ] Checked on closures/mandates that might affect your travel?
- [ ] ⋯⋯⋯⋯⋯⋯⋯
- [ ] ⋯⋯⋯⋯⋯⋯⋯
- [ ] ⋯⋯⋯⋯⋯⋯⋯

MAIN GOALS

- [ ] Solitude
- [ ] Active adventure
- [ ] Creative pursuits
- [ ] Learning
- [ ] Endurance training
- [ ] Gathering loved ones
- [ ] Seeing new things!
- [ ] ⋯⋯⋯⋯⋯⋯⋯
- [ ] ⋯⋯⋯⋯⋯⋯⋯
- [ ] ⋯⋯⋯⋯⋯⋯⋯

IMMERSIVE EXPERIENCES

- [ ] Cultural/historical
- [ ] Volunteering
- [ ] Park programs
- [ ] Junior Ranger program
- [ ] NPS-guided night walks
- [ ] School/youth trips
- [ ] Teacher/educator programs
- [ ] Professional development
- [ ] ⋯⋯⋯⋯⋯⋯⋯
- [ ] ⋯⋯⋯⋯⋯⋯⋯
- [ ] ⋯⋯⋯⋯⋯⋯⋯

ADVENTURE GOALS

- [ ] Hiking big trails
- [ ] Easy day hikes
- [ ] Cycling/mountain biking/fat biking
- [ ] Kayaking/canoeing/SUP
- [ ] Trail running
- [ ] Rafting
- [ ] Swimming
- [ ] Backpacking
- [ ] Wildlife viewing
- [ ] Scenic drives
- [ ] Fishing/angling
- [ ] Mountaineering
- [ ] Climbing/bouldering
- [ ] Photography
- [ ] Birdwatching
- [ ] Stargazing
- [ ] Cultural immersion
- [ ] Endurance training
- [ ] Picnicking
- [ ] ⋯⋯⋯⋯⋯⋯⋯

PHOTOGRAPHY PLANS

- [ ] Wildlife
- [ ] Birds
- [ ] Landscapes
- [ ] Night skies
- [ ] People
- [ ] Cultural artifacts
- [ ] Macro/abstract
- [ ] Family pictures
- [ ] Selfies
- [ ] ⋯⋯⋯⋯⋯⋯⋯

ADDITIONAL NOTES

⋯⋯⋯⋯⋯⋯⋯
⋯⋯⋯⋯⋯⋯⋯
⋯⋯⋯⋯⋯⋯⋯
⋯⋯⋯⋯⋯⋯⋯

PACK FOR YOUR TRIP!

Park name: ....

HEALTH & PERSONAL ITEMS
- [ ] Premade first aid kit
- [ ] Wildlife/insect protection
- [ ] Medications
- [ ] ....
- [ ] ....
- [ ] Supplements
- [ ] ....
- [ ] ....
- [ ] Eyeglasses/contacts
- [ ] Sun/wind/snow protection (eyes/skin/face)
- [ ] Facial tissues
- [ ] Bug spray
- [ ] Antibacterial wipes
- [ ] ....
- [ ] ....

ELECTRONICS
- [ ] Camera
  - [ ] Tripod
  - [ ] Lenses/lens cloths
  - [ ] Memory cards
  - [ ] Batteries & charger
- [ ] Weather protection
- [ ] External charging device
- [ ] Phone & charging cord
- [ ] Mobile Wi-Fi device
- [ ] Electronic tablet
- [ ] Satellite phone
- [ ] Personal locater beacon
- [ ] ....

CLOTHING/SHOES
- [ ] Insulated jacket
- [ ] Rain jacket/pants
- [ ] Thermal layers
- [ ] Wicked/quick-dry clothing
- [ ] Loose-fitting shirts
- [ ] Loose-fitting pants
- [ ] Hiking pants/shorts
- [ ] Short-sleeved/sleeveless shirts
- [ ] Full winter gear
- [ ] ....
- [ ] ....
- [ ] ....
- [ ] Leisurewear
- [ ] Beachwear
- [ ] Hiking shoes
- [ ] Athletic shoes
- [ ] Water shoes
- [ ] Sandals/flip-flops
- [ ] Neck gaiter
- [ ] Sun hat/cap
- [ ] Stocking cap
- [ ] Socks + extra pair
- [ ] Undergarments
- [ ] Gloves/mittens
- [ ] ....
- [ ] ....
- [ ] ....
- [ ] ....
- [ ] ....
- [ ] ....
- [ ] ....

OUTDOOR GEAR
- [ ] Hiking poles
- [ ] Tent
- [ ] Sleeping bag
- [ ] Sleeping pad
- [ ] Pillow
- [ ] Shade tent
- [ ] Emergency space blanket
- [ ] Tarp
- [ ] Daypack
- [ ] Headlamp(s)
- [ ] Lantern(s)
- [ ] Water filter & iodine tablets
- [ ] Large refillable water jug
- [ ] Portable stove
- [ ] Hot beverage thermos
- [ ] Nylon hammock
- [ ] Throw blanket
- [ ] Reusable dishes/cutlery
- [ ] Hand warmers
- [ ] ....
- [ ] ....
- [ ] ....
- [ ] ....
- [ ] ....
- [ ] ....
- [ ] ....
- [ ] ....
- [ ] ....
- [ ] ....

FOOD & DRINK

- [ ] Water
- [ ] Refillable water bottle
- [ ] Energy drinks with electrolytes
- [ ] Protein-packed snacks
- [ ] Salty, easy-to-digest snacks
- [ ] Dehydrated food
- [ ] No-cook food items
- [ ] ....
- [ ] ....
- [ ] ....
- [ ] ....
- [ ] ....
- [ ] ....
- [ ] ....
- [ ] ....
- [ ] ....
- [ ] ....
- [ ] ....
- [ ] ....
- [ ] ....
- [ ] ....

PARK-SPECIFIC

- [ ] *The National Parks Journal*!
- [ ] Permits
- [ ] Guidebooks
- [ ] Park map
- [ ] ....
- [ ] ....
- [ ] ....
- [ ] ....
- [ ] ....
- [ ] ....
- [ ] ....

MISCELLANEOUS

- [ ] Duct tape
- [ ] Multipurpose tool
- [ ] Knife
- [ ] Scissors
- [ ] Can opener
- [ ] Matches/lighter/firestarter
- [ ] Hatchet
- [ ] Whistle
- [ ] Bandana
- [ ] Quick-dry towels
- [ ] Waterproof bags
- [ ] Ziplock bags
- [ ] Trash bags
- [ ] Paper towels
- [ ] Bear can
- [ ] Binoculars
- [ ] Deck of cards/games
- [ ] Driver's license, registration, insurance, etc.
- [ ] Spare tire/jack
- [ ] Wiper blades
- [ ] Small amount of cash
- [ ] ....
- [ ] ....
- [ ] ....
- [ ] ....
- [ ] ....
- [ ] ....
- [ ] ....
- [ ] ....
- [ ] ....
- [ ] ....
- [ ] ....
- [ ] ....
- [ ] ....
- [ ] ....

PERSONALIZED LIST

- [ ] ....
- [ ] ....
- [ ] ....
- [ ] ....
- [ ] ....
- [ ] ....
- [ ] ....
- [ ] ....
- [ ] ....
- [ ] ....

TO BUY

- [ ] ....
- [ ] ....
- [ ] ....
- [ ] ....
- [ ] ....
- [ ] ....
- [ ] ....
- [ ] ....
- [ ] ....
- [ ] ....

ADDITIONAL NOTES

....
....
....
....
....
....
....
....
....
....
....
....
....
....

RECORD YOUR TRIP!

Park name: ....

State/territory: ....

Dates visited: ....

Nearby sites visited: ....

5 — Epic & life-changing experience

4 — Want to learn everything about this park!

3 — See why this place is so special

2 — Happy I went and had some good times

1 — Once and done!

FAVORITE CAMPSITE OR LODGING: ....

....

PEAK EXPERIENCE: ....

....

FAVORITE ADVENTURE: ....

....

FAVORITE LOCATION: ....

....

FAVORITE PHOTO: ....

....

BEST WILDLIFE SIGHTING: ....

....

FUN THING(S) I LEARNED ABOUT THE PARK: ....

....

INTERESTING PEOPLE MET ALONG MY JOURNEY:

VALUABLE RESOURCE(S) DISCOVERED ALONG THE WAY:

FOOD I COULDN'T LIVE WITHOUT:

THE BIGGEST CHALLENGE I FACED:

I WAS MOST PREPARED WHEN:

WISH I KNEW BEFORE I WENT:

WISH I WOULD HAVE BROUGHT:

MOST USEFUL PIECE OF GEAR:

MOST VALUABLE TOOL:

MOST USEFUL PIECE OF ADVICE:

TIPS FOR OTHER TRAVELERS:

ADDITIONAL NOTES:

PLAN YOUR TRIP!

Park name: ....

State/territory: .... Temperature range: ....

Planned dates: .... Altitude range: ....

Time zone: .... Latitude/longitude: ....

COMMITMENT LEVEL

- 6 — Full throttle, all-in adventure time!
- 5 — Bring on a big challenge!
- 4 — Many trails, sites, & adventures planned!
- 3 — Rolling where the wind blows me!
- 2 — Tons to do without breaking a big sweat!
- 1 — Easy-going, leisurely days...

SEASON OF VISIT
- ☐ Spring
- ☐ Summer
- ☐ Autumn
- ☐ Winter

TOURING/SUPPORT
- ☐ Self-guided
- ☐ Privately guided
- ☐ Chartered trip
- ☐ Group trip
- ☐ Volunteering
- ☐ Ranger-led tours
- ☐ Instructional classes
- ☐ Special events
- ....
- ....
- ....
- ....
- ....

PARK TRANSPORT
- ☐ Car
- ☐ Bus
- ☐ RV/travel trailer
- ☐ Boat
- ☐ Float plane/bush plane
- ☐ Helicopter
- ☐ Tour bus
- ☐ All-terrain vehicle
- ☐ ....

PARK ITEMS TO PICK UP
- ☐ NPS annual pass
- ☐ NPS parks passport
- ☐ Pins, patches, & stickers
- ☐ Hiking stick medallions
- ☐ NPS maps & literature
- ☐ ....
- ☐ ....
- ☐ ....

RESOURCES/CONTACTS
- ☐ NPS visitor center(s):
- ....
- ☐ Wilderness permit(s):
- ....
- ☐ Tour company:
- ....
- ☐ Local guide(s):
- ....
- ☐ Local gear outfitter(s):
- ....
- ☐ Emergency services:
- ....
- ☐ Miscellaneous contact:
- ....
- ☐ Miscellaneous contact:
- ....

MAIN ACCOMMODATIONS
- ☐ NPS lodge
- ☐ Hotel
- ☐ RV/travel trailer
- ☐ Tent camping
- ☐ Backcountry camping
- ☐ Staying with friends
- ☐ Houseboat
- ☐ Cruise ship
- ☐ Van/car
- ☐ ....
- ☐ ....

AMENITIES

- [ ] Campgrounds
  - [ ] Standard
  - [ ] RV
  - [ ] Primitive
  - [ ] Day use only
  - [ ] Group
- [ ] Plumbed bathrooms
- [ ] Showers
- [ ] Park store
- [ ] Wi-Fi
- [ ] NPS amphitheater
- [ ] Pet-friendly
- [ ] ----------------------------------
- [ ] ----------------------------------

IN-TOW

- [ ] Spouse/partner
- [ ] Children
- [ ] Pets
- [ ] Friends
- [ ] Extended family
- [ ] Boatloads of gear!
- [ ] ----------------------------------
- [ ] ----------------------------------

ADVANCED PLANNING

- [ ] Physical training?

- [ ] Seasonal aspects?

- [ ] Obtained permits?

- [ ] Purchased gear?

FINAL SAFETY CHECKS

- [ ] Left your trip plan with an emergency contact back home?
- [ ] Reviewed basic emergency aid procedures?
- [ ] Additional forms/permits needed?
- [ ] Checked on closures/mandates that might affect your travel?
- [ ] ----------------------------------
- [ ] ----------------------------------
- [ ] ----------------------------------

MAIN GOALS

- [ ] Solitude
- [ ] Active adventure
- [ ] Creative pursuits
- [ ] Learning
- [ ] Endurance training
- [ ] Gathering loved ones
- [ ] Seeing new things!
- [ ] ----------------------------------
- [ ] ----------------------------------
- [ ] ----------------------------------

IMMERSIVE EXPERIENCES

- [ ] Cultural/historical
- [ ] Volunteering
- [ ] Park programs
- [ ] Junior Ranger program
- [ ] NPS-guided night walks
- [ ] School/youth trips
- [ ] Teacher/educator programs
- [ ] Professional development
- [ ] ----------------------------------
- [ ] ----------------------------------
- [ ] ----------------------------------

ADVENTURE GOALS

- [ ] Hiking big trails
- [ ] Easy day hikes
- [ ] Cycling/mountain biking/fat biking
- [ ] Kayaking/canoeing/SUP
- [ ] Trail running
- [ ] Rafting
- [ ] Swimming
- [ ] Backpacking
- [ ] Wildlife viewing
- [ ] Scenic drives
- [ ] Fishing/angling
- [ ] Mountaineering
- [ ] Climbing/bouldering
- [ ] Photography
- [ ] Birdwatching
- [ ] Stargazing
- [ ] Cultural immersion
- [ ] Endurance training
- [ ] Picnicking
- [ ] ----------------------------------

PHOTOGRAPHY PLANS

- [ ] Wildlife
- [ ] Birds
- [ ] Landscapes
- [ ] Night skies
- [ ] People
- [ ] Cultural artifacts
- [ ] Macro/abstract
- [ ] Family pictures
- [ ] Selfies
- [ ] ----------------------------------

ADDITIONAL NOTES

PACK FOR YOUR TRIP!

Park name: ....

HEALTH & PERSONAL ITEMS

- [ ] Premade first aid kit
- [ ] Wildlife/insect protection
- [ ] Medications
  - ....
  - ....
- [ ] Supplements
  - ....
  - ....
- [ ] Eyeglasses/contacts
- [ ] Sun/wind/snow protection (eyes/skin/face)
- [ ] Facial tissues
- [ ] Bug spray
- [ ] Antibacterial wipes
- [ ] ....
- [ ] ....

ELECTRONICS

- [ ] Camera
  - [ ] Tripod
  - [ ] Lenses/lens cloths
  - [ ] Memory cards
  - [ ] Batteries & charger
- [ ] Weather protection
- [ ] External charging device
- [ ] Phone & charging cord
- [ ] Mobile Wi-Fi device
- [ ] Electronic tablet
- [ ] Satellite phone
- [ ] Personal locater beacon
- [ ] ....

CLOTHING/SHOES

- [ ] Insulated jacket
- [ ] Rain jacket/pants
- [ ] Thermal layers
- [ ] Wicked/quick-dry clothing
- [ ] Loose-fitting shirts
- [ ] Loose-fitting pants
- [ ] Hiking pants/shorts
- [ ] Short-sleeved/sleeveless shirts
- [ ] Full winter gear
  - ....
  - ....
  - ....
- [ ] Leisurewear
- [ ] Beachwear
- [ ] Hiking shoes
- [ ] Athletic shoes
- [ ] Water shoes
- [ ] Sandals/flip-flops
- [ ] Neck gaiter
- [ ] Sun hat/cap
- [ ] Stocking cap
- [ ] Socks + extra pair
- [ ] Undergarments
- [ ] Gloves/mittens
- [ ] ....
- [ ] ....
- [ ] ....
- [ ] ....
- [ ] ....
- [ ] ....
- [ ] ....
- [ ] ....

OUTDOOR GEAR

- [ ] Hiking poles
- [ ] Tent
- [ ] Sleeping bag
- [ ] Sleeping pad
- [ ] Pillow
- [ ] Shade tent
- [ ] Emergency space blanket
- [ ] Tarp
- [ ] Daypack
- [ ] Headlamp(s)
- [ ] Lantern(s)
- [ ] Water filter & iodine tablets
- [ ] Large refillable water jug
- [ ] Portable stove
- [ ] Hot beverage thermos
- [ ] Nylon hammock
- [ ] Throw blanket
- [ ] Reusable dishes/cutlery
- [ ] Hand warmers
- [ ] ....
- [ ] ....
- [ ] ....
- [ ] ....
- [ ] ....
- [ ] ....
- [ ] ....
- [ ] ....
- [ ] ....
- [ ] ....
- [ ] ....

FOOD & DRINK

- [ ] Water
- [ ] Refillable water bottle
- [ ] Energy drinks with electrolytes
- [ ] Protein-packed snacks
- [ ] Salty, easy-to-digest snacks
- [ ] Dehydrated food
- [ ] No-cook food items
- [ ] ....
- [ ] ....
- [ ] ....
- [ ] ....
- [ ] ....
- [ ] ....
- [ ] ....
- [ ] ....
- [ ] ....
- [ ] ....
- [ ] ....
- [ ] ....
- [ ] ....
- [ ] ....

PARK-SPECIFIC

- [ ] *The National Parks Journal*!
- [ ] Permits
- [ ] Guidebooks
- [ ] Park map
- [ ] ....
- [ ] ....
- [ ] ....
- [ ] ....
- [ ] ....
- [ ] ....

MISCELLANEOUS

- [ ] Duct tape
- [ ] Multipurpose tool
- [ ] Knife
- [ ] Scissors
- [ ] Can opener
- [ ] Matches/lighter/ firestarter
- [ ] Hatchet
- [ ] Whistle
- [ ] Bandana
- [ ] Quick-dry towels
- [ ] Waterproof bags
- [ ] Ziplock bags
- [ ] Trash bags
- [ ] Paper towels
- [ ] Bear can
- [ ] Binoculars
- [ ] Deck of cards/games
- [ ] Driver's license, registration, insurance, etc.
- [ ] Spare tire/jack
- [ ] Wiper blades
- [ ] Small amount of cash
- [ ] ....
- [ ] ....
- [ ] ....
- [ ] ....
- [ ] ....
- [ ] ....
- [ ] ....
- [ ] ....
- [ ] ....
- [ ] ....
- [ ] ....
- [ ] ....
- [ ] ....
- [ ] ....
- [ ] ....
- [ ] ....

PERSONALIZED LIST

- [ ] ....
- [ ] ....
- [ ] ....
- [ ] ....
- [ ] ....
- [ ] ....
- [ ] ....
- [ ] ....
- [ ] ....
- [ ] ....

TO BUY

- [ ] ....
- [ ] ....
- [ ] ....
- [ ] ....
- [ ] ....
- [ ] ....
- [ ] ....
- [ ] ....
- [ ] ....
- [ ] ....

ADDITIONAL NOTES

RECORD YOUR TRIP!

Park name: ....

State/territory: ....

Dates visited: ....

Nearby sites visited: ....

ARROWHEAD RATING!

- 5 — Epic & life-changing experience
- 4 — Want to learn everything about this park!
- 3 — See why this place is so special
- 2 — Happy I went and had some good times
- 1 — Once and done!

FAVORITE CAMPSITE OR LODGING: ....

....

PEAK EXPERIENCE: ....

....

FAVORITE ADVENTURE: ....

....

FAVORITE LOCATION: ....

....

FAVORITE PHOTO: ....

....

BEST WILDLIFE SIGHTING: ....

....

FUN THING(S) I LEARNED ABOUT THE PARK: ....

....

INTERESTING PEOPLE MET ALONG MY JOURNEY: ....

....

VALUABLE RESOURCE(S) DISCOVERED ALONG THE WAY: ....

....

FOOD I COULDN'T LIVE WITHOUT: ....

....

THE BIGGEST CHALLENGE I FACED: ....

....

I WAS MOST PREPARED WHEN: ....

....

WISH I KNEW BEFORE I WENT: ....

....

WISH I WOULD HAVE BROUGHT: ....

....

MOST USEFUL PIECE OF GEAR: ....

....

MOST VALUABLE TOOL: ....

....

MOST USEFUL PIECE OF ADVICE: ....

....

TIPS FOR OTHER TRAVELERS: ....

....

ADDITIONAL NOTES: ....

....

....

....

....

PLAN YOUR TRIP!

Park name: ....

State/territory: ....   Temperature range: ....

Planned dates: ....   Altitude range: ....

Time zone: ....   Latitude/longitude: ....

COMMITMENT LEVEL

⬦ 6 — Full throttle, all-in adventure time!

⬦ 5 — Bring on a big challenge!

⬦ 4 — Many trails, sites, & adventures planned!

⬦ 3 — Rolling where the wind blows me!

⬦ 2 — Tons to do without breaking a big sweat!

⬦ 1 — Easy-going, leisurely days...

SEASON OF VISIT

☐ Spring
☐ Summer
☐ Autumn
☐ Winter

TOURING/SUPPORT

☐ Self-guided
☐ Privately guided
☐ Chartered trip
☐ Group trip
☐ Volunteering
☐ Ranger-led tours
☐ Instructional classes
☐ Special events
....
....
....
....
....

PARK TRANSPORT

☐ Car
☐ Bus
☐ RV/travel trailer
☐ Boat
☐ Float plane/bush plane
☐ Helicopter
☐ Tour bus
☐ All-terrain vehicle
☐ ....

PARK ITEMS TO PICK UP

☐ NPS annual pass
☐ NPS parks passport
☐ Pins, patches, & stickers
☐ Hiking stick medallions
☐ NPS maps & literature
☐ ....
☐ ....
☐ ....

RESOURCES/CONTACTS

☐ NPS visitor center(s):
....
☐ Wilderness permit(s):
....
☐ Tour company:
....
☐ Local guide(s):
....
☐ Local gear outfitter(s):
....
☐ Emergency services:
....
☐ Miscellaneous contact:
....
☐ Miscellaneous contact:
....

MAIN ACCOMMODATIONS

☐ NPS lodge
☐ Hotel
☐ RV/travel trailer
☐ Tent camping
☐ Backcountry camping
☐ Staying with friends
☐ Houseboat
☐ Cruise ship
☐ Van/car
☐ ....
☐ ....

AMENITIES

- [ ] Campgrounds
  - [ ] Standard
  - [ ] RV
  - [ ] Primitive
  - [ ] Day use only
  - [ ] Group
- [ ] Plumbed bathrooms
- [ ] Showers
- [ ] Park store
- [ ] Wi-Fi
- [ ] NPS amphitheater
- [ ] Pet-friendly
- [ ] ----------------------------
- [ ] ----------------------------

IN-TOW

- [ ] Spouse/partner
- [ ] Children
- [ ] Pets
- [ ] Friends
- [ ] Extended family
- [ ] Boatloads of gear!
- [ ] ----------------------------
- [ ] ----------------------------

ADVANCED PLANNING

- [ ] Physical training?

- [ ] Seasonal aspects?

- [ ] Obtained permits?

- [ ] Purchased gear?

FINAL SAFETY CHECKS

- [ ] Left your trip plan with an emergency contact back home?
- [ ] Reviewed basic emergency aid procedures?
- [ ] Additional forms/permits needed?
- [ ] Checked on closures/mandates that might affect your travel?
- [ ] ----------------------------
- [ ] ----------------------------
- [ ] ----------------------------

MAIN GOALS

- [ ] Solitude
- [ ] Active adventure
- [ ] Creative pursuits
- [ ] Learning
- [ ] Endurance training
- [ ] Gathering loved ones
- [ ] Seeing new things!
- [ ] ----------------------------
- [ ] ----------------------------
- [ ] ----------------------------

IMMERSIVE EXPERIENCES

- [ ] Cultural/historical
- [ ] Volunteering
- [ ] Park programs
- [ ] Junior Ranger program
- [ ] NPS-guided night walks
- [ ] School/youth trips
- [ ] Teacher/educator programs
- [ ] Professional development
- [ ] ----------------------------
- [ ] ----------------------------
- [ ] ----------------------------

ADVENTURE GOALS

- [ ] Hiking big trails
- [ ] Easy day hikes
- [ ] Cycling/mountain biking/fat biking
- [ ] Kayaking/canoeing/SUP
- [ ] Trail running
- [ ] Rafting
- [ ] Swimming
- [ ] Backpacking
- [ ] Wildlife viewing
- [ ] Scenic drives
- [ ] Fishing/angling
- [ ] Mountaineering
- [ ] Climbing/bouldering
- [ ] Photography
- [ ] Birdwatching
- [ ] Stargazing
- [ ] Cultural immersion
- [ ] Endurance training
- [ ] Picnicking
- [ ] ----------------------------

PHOTOGRAPHY PLANS

- [ ] Wildlife
- [ ] Birds
- [ ] Landscapes
- [ ] Night skies
- [ ] People
- [ ] Cultural artifacts
- [ ] Macro/abstract
- [ ] Family pictures
- [ ] Selfies
- [ ] ----------------------------

ADDITIONAL NOTES

PACK FOR YOUR TRIP!

Park name: ....

HEALTH & PERSONAL ITEMS
- [ ] Premade first aid kit
- [ ] Wildlife/insect protection
- [ ] Medications
  - ----------------------------------
  - ----------------------------------
- [ ] Supplements
  - ----------------------------------
  - ----------------------------------
- [ ] Eyeglasses/contacts
- [ ] Sun/wind/snow protection (eyes/skin/face)
- [ ] Facial tissues
- [ ] Bug spray
- [ ] Antibacterial wipes
- [ ] ----------------------------------
- [ ] ----------------------------------

ELECTRONICS
- [ ] Camera
  - [ ] Tripod
  - [ ] Lenses/lens cloths
  - [ ] Memory cards
  - [ ] Batteries & charger
- [ ] Weather protection
- [ ] External charging device
- [ ] Phone & charging cord
- [ ] Mobile Wi-Fi device
- [ ] Electronic tablet
- [ ] Satellite phone
- [ ] Personal locater beacon
- [ ] ----------------------------------

CLOTHING/SHOES
- [ ] Insulated jacket
- [ ] Rain jacket/pants
- [ ] Thermal layers
- [ ] Wicked/quick-dry clothing
- [ ] Loose-fitting shirts
- [ ] Loose-fitting pants
- [ ] Hiking pants/shorts
- [ ] Short-sleeved/sleeveless shirts
- [ ] Full winter gear
  - ----------------------------------
  - ----------------------------------
  - ----------------------------------
- [ ] Leisurewear
- [ ] Beachwear
- [ ] Hiking shoes
- [ ] Athletic shoes
- [ ] Water shoes
- [ ] Sandals/flip-flops
- [ ] Neck gaiter
- [ ] Sun hat/cap
- [ ] Stocking cap
- [ ] Socks + extra pair
- [ ] Undergarments
- [ ] Gloves/mittens
- [ ] ----------------------------------
- [ ] ----------------------------------
- [ ] ----------------------------------
- [ ] ----------------------------------
- [ ] ----------------------------------
- [ ] ----------------------------------
- [ ] ----------------------------------

OUTDOOR GEAR
- [ ] Hiking poles
- [ ] Tent
- [ ] Sleeping bag
- [ ] Sleeping pad
- [ ] Pillow
- [ ] Shade tent
- [ ] Emergency space blanket
- [ ] Tarp
- [ ] Daypack
- [ ] Headlamp(s)
- [ ] Lantern(s)
- [ ] Water filter & iodine tablets
- [ ] Large refillable water jug
- [ ] Portable stove
- [ ] Hot beverage thermos
- [ ] Nylon hammock
- [ ] Throw blanket
- [ ] Reusable dishes/cutlery
- [ ] Hand warmers
- [ ] ----------------------------------
- [ ] ----------------------------------
- [ ] ----------------------------------
- [ ] ----------------------------------
- [ ] ----------------------------------
- [ ] ----------------------------------
- [ ] ----------------------------------
- [ ] ----------------------------------
- [ ] ----------------------------------
- [ ] ----------------------------------
- [ ] ----------------------------------

FOOD & DRINK

- [ ] Water
- [ ] Refillable water bottle
- [ ] Energy drinks with electrolytes
- [ ] Protein-packed snacks
- [ ] Salty, easy-to-digest snacks
- [ ] Dehydrated food
- [ ] No-cook food items
- [ ] ....
- [ ] ....
- [ ] ....
- [ ] ....
- [ ] ....
- [ ] ....
- [ ] ....
- [ ] ....
- [ ] ....
- [ ] ....
- [ ] ....
- [ ] ....
- [ ] ....
- [ ] ....
- [ ] ....

PARK-SPECIFIC

- [ ] *The National Parks Journal*!
- [ ] Permits
- [ ] Guidebooks
- [ ] Park map
- [ ] ....
- [ ] ....
- [ ] ....
- [ ] ....
- [ ] ....
- [ ] ....
- [ ] ....

MISCELLANEOUS

- [ ] Duct tape
- [ ] Multipurpose tool
- [ ] Knife
- [ ] Scissors
- [ ] Can opener
- [ ] Matches/lighter/firestarter
- [ ] Hatchet
- [ ] Whistle
- [ ] Bandana
- [ ] Quick-dry towels
- [ ] Waterproof bags
- [ ] Ziplock bags
- [ ] Trash bags
- [ ] Paper towels
- [ ] Bear can
- [ ] Binoculars
- [ ] Deck of cards/games
- [ ] Driver's license, registration, insurance, etc.
- [ ] Spare tire/jack
- [ ] Wiper blades
- [ ] Small amount of cash
- [ ] ....
- [ ] ....
- [ ] ....
- [ ] ....
- [ ] ....
- [ ] ....
- [ ] ....
- [ ] ....
- [ ] ....
- [ ] ....
- [ ] ....
- [ ] ....
- [ ] ....
- [ ] ....
- [ ] ....

PERSONALIZED LIST

- [ ] ....
- [ ] ....
- [ ] ....
- [ ] ....
- [ ] ....
- [ ] ....
- [ ] ....
- [ ] ....
- [ ] ....
- [ ] ....

TO BUY

- [ ] ....
- [ ] ....
- [ ] ....
- [ ] ....
- [ ] ....
- [ ] ....
- [ ] ....
- [ ] ....
- [ ] ....
- [ ] ....

ADDITIONAL NOTES

RECORD YOUR TRIP!

Park name: ....

State/territory: ....

Dates visited: ....

Nearby sites visited: ....

ARROWHEAD RATING!

5 — Epic & life-changing experience
4 — Want to learn everything about this park!
3 — See why this place is so special
2 — Happy I went and had some good times
1 — Once and done!

FAVORITE CAMPSITE OR LODGING: ....

....

PEAK EXPERIENCE: ....

....

FAVORITE ADVENTURE: ....

....

FAVORITE LOCATION: ....

....

FAVORITE PHOTO: ....

....

BEST WILDLIFE SIGHTING: ....

....

FUN THING(S) I LEARNED ABOUT THE PARK: ....

....

INTERESTING PEOPLE MET ALONG MY JOURNEY: --

VALUABLE RESOURCE(S) DISCOVERED ALONG THE WAY: ---

FOOD I COULDN'T LIVE WITHOUT: --

THE BIGGEST CHALLENGE I FACED: ---

I WAS MOST PREPARED WHEN: --

WISH I KNEW BEFORE I WENT: --

WISH I WOULD HAVE BROUGHT: --

MOST USEFUL PIECE OF GEAR: --

MOST VALUABLE TOOL: ---

MOST USEFUL PIECE OF ADVICE: ---

TIPS FOR OTHER TRAVELERS: ---

ADDITIONAL NOTES: --

PLAN YOUR TRIP!

Park name: ....

State/territory: ....   Temperature range: ....

Planned dates: ....   Altitude range: ....

Time zone: ....   Latitude/longitude: ....

COMMITMENT LEVEL

- 6 — Full throttle, all-in adventure time!
- 5 — Bring on a big challenge!
- 4 — Many trails, sites, & adventures planned!
- 3 — Rolling where the wind blows me!
- 2 — Tons to do without breaking a big sweat!
- 1 — Easy-going, leisurely days...

SEASON OF VISIT

- ☐ Spring
- ☐ Summer
- ☐ Autumn
- ☐ Winter

TOURING/SUPPORT

- ☐ Self-guided
- ☐ Privately guided
- ☐ Chartered trip
- ☐ Group trip
- ☐ Volunteering
- ☐ Ranger-led tours
- ☐ Instructional classes
- ☐ Special events
- ....
- ....
- ....
- ....
- ....

PARK TRANSPORT

- ☐ Car
- ☐ Bus
- ☐ RV/travel trailer
- ☐ Boat
- ☐ Float plane/bush plane
- ☐ Helicopter
- ☐ Tour bus
- ☐ All-terrain vehicle
- ☐ ....

PARK ITEMS TO PICK UP

- ☐ NPS annual pass
- ☐ NPS parks passport
- ☐ Pins, patches, & stickers
- ☐ Hiking stick medallions
- ☐ NPS maps & literature
- ☐ ....
- ☐ ....
- ☐ ....

RESOURCES/CONTACTS

- ☐ NPS visitor center(s):

- ☐ Wilderness permit(s):

- ☐ Tour company:

- ☐ Local guide(s):

- ☐ Local gear outfitter(s):

- ☐ Emergency services:

- ☐ Miscellaneous contact:

- ☐ Miscellaneous contact:

MAIN ACCOMMODATIONS

- ☐ NPS lodge
- ☐ Hotel
- ☐ RV/travel trailer
- ☐ Tent camping
- ☐ Backcountry camping
- ☐ Staying with friends
- ☐ Houseboat
- ☐ Cruise ship
- ☐ Van/car
- ☐ ....
- ☐ ....

AMENITIES

- [ ] Campgrounds
  - [ ] Standard
  - [ ] RV
  - [ ] Primitive
  - [ ] Day use only
  - [ ] Group
- [ ] Plumbed bathrooms
- [ ] Showers
- [ ] Park store
- [ ] Wi-Fi
- [ ] NPS amphitheater
- [ ] Pet-friendly
- [ ] ....
- [ ] ....

IN-TOW

- [ ] Spouse/partner
- [ ] Children
- [ ] Pets
- [ ] Friends
- [ ] Extended family
- [ ] Boatloads of gear!
- [ ] ....
- [ ] ....

ADVANCED PLANNING

- [ ] Physical training?

....

....

- [ ] Seasonal aspects?

....

....

- [ ] Obtained permits?

....

....

- [ ] Purchased gear?

....

....

....

FINAL SAFETY CHECKS

- [ ] Left your trip plan with an emergency contact back home?
- [ ] Reviewed basic emergency aid procedures?
- [ ] Additional forms/permits needed?
- [ ] Checked on closures/mandates that might affect your travel?
- [ ] ....
- [ ] ....
- [ ] ....

MAIN GOALS

- [ ] Solitude
- [ ] Active adventure
- [ ] Creative pursuits
- [ ] Learning
- [ ] Endurance training
- [ ] Gathering loved ones
- [ ] Seeing new things!
- [ ] ....
- [ ] ....
- [ ] ....

IMMERSIVE EXPERIENCES

- [ ] Cultural/historical
- [ ] Volunteering
- [ ] Park programs
- [ ] Junior Ranger program
- [ ] NPS-guided night walks
- [ ] School/youth trips
- [ ] Teacher/educator programs
- [ ] Professional development
- [ ] ....
- [ ] ....
- [ ] ....

ADVENTURE GOALS

- [ ] Hiking big trails
- [ ] Easy day hikes
- [ ] Cycling/mountain biking/fat biking
- [ ] Kayaking/canoeing/SUP
- [ ] Trail running
- [ ] Rafting
- [ ] Swimming
- [ ] Backpacking
- [ ] Wildlife viewing
- [ ] Scenic drives
- [ ] Fishing/angling
- [ ] Mountaineering
- [ ] Climbing/bouldering
- [ ] Photography
- [ ] Birdwatching
- [ ] Stargazing
- [ ] Cultural immersion
- [ ] Endurance training
- [ ] Picnicking
- [ ] ....

PHOTOGRAPHY PLANS

- [ ] Wildlife
- [ ] Birds
- [ ] Landscapes
- [ ] Night skies
- [ ] People
- [ ] Cultural artifacts
- [ ] Macro/abstract
- [ ] Family pictures
- [ ] Selfies
- [ ] ....

ADDITIONAL NOTES

....

....

....

....

PACK FOR YOUR TRIP!

Park name: ....

HEALTH & PERSONAL ITEMS
- [ ] Premade first aid kit
- [ ] Wildlife/insect protection
- [ ] Medications
- [ ] ....
- [ ] ....
- [ ] Supplements
- [ ] ....
- [ ] ....
- [ ] Eyeglasses/contacts
- [ ] Sun/wind/snow protection (eyes/skin/face)
- [ ] Facial tissues
- [ ] Bug spray
- [ ] Antibacterial wipes
- [ ] ....
- [ ] ....

ELECTRONICS
- [ ] Camera
  - [ ] Tripod
  - [ ] Lenses/lens cloths
  - [ ] Memory cards
  - [ ] Batteries & charger
- [ ] Weather protection
- [ ] External charging device
- [ ] Phone & charging cord
- [ ] Mobile Wi-Fi device
- [ ] Electronic tablet
- [ ] Satellite phone
- [ ] Personal locater beacon
- [ ] ....

CLOTHING/SHOES
- [ ] Insulated jacket
- [ ] Rain jacket/pants
- [ ] Thermal layers
- [ ] Wicked/quick-dry clothing
- [ ] Loose-fitting shirts
- [ ] Loose-fitting pants
- [ ] Hiking pants/shorts
- [ ] Short-sleeved/sleeveless shirts
- [ ] Full winter gear
- [ ] ....
- [ ] ....
- [ ] ....
- [ ] Leisurewear
- [ ] Beachwear
- [ ] Hiking shoes
- [ ] Athletic shoes
- [ ] Water shoes
- [ ] Sandals/flip-flops
- [ ] Neck gaiter
- [ ] Sun hat/cap
- [ ] Stocking cap
- [ ] Socks + extra pair
- [ ] Undergarments
- [ ] Gloves/mittens
- [ ] ....
- [ ] ....
- [ ] ....
- [ ] ....
- [ ] ....
- [ ] ....
- [ ] ....
- [ ] ....

OUTDOOR GEAR
- [ ] Hiking poles
- [ ] Tent
- [ ] Sleeping bag
- [ ] Sleeping pad
- [ ] Pillow
- [ ] Shade tent
- [ ] Emergency space blanket
- [ ] Tarp
- [ ] Daypack
- [ ] Headlamp(s)
- [ ] Lantern(s)
- [ ] Water filter & iodine tablets
- [ ] Large refillable water jug
- [ ] Portable stove
- [ ] Hot beverage thermos
- [ ] Nylon hammock
- [ ] Throw blanket
- [ ] Reusable dishes/cutlery
- [ ] Hand warmers
- [ ] ....
- [ ] ....
- [ ] ....
- [ ] ....
- [ ] ....
- [ ] ....
- [ ] ....
- [ ] ....

FOOD & DRINK

- [ ] Water
- [ ] Refillable water bottle
- [ ] Energy drinks with electrolytes
- [ ] Protein-packed snacks
- [ ] Salty, easy-to-digest snacks
- [ ] Dehydrated food
- [ ] No-cook food items
- [ ] ....
- [ ] ....
- [ ] ....
- [ ] ....
- [ ] ....
- [ ] ....
- [ ] ....
- [ ] ....
- [ ] ....
- [ ] ....
- [ ] ....
- [ ] ....
- [ ] ....
- [ ] ....

PARK-SPECIFIC

- [ ] *The National Parks Journal*!
- [ ] Permits
- [ ] Guidebooks
- [ ] Park map
- [ ] ....
- [ ] ....
- [ ] ....
- [ ] ....
- [ ] ....
- [ ] ....
- [ ] ....

MISCELLANEOUS

- [ ] Duct tape
- [ ] Multipurpose tool
- [ ] Knife
- [ ] Scissors
- [ ] Can opener
- [ ] Matches/lighter/firestarter
- [ ] Hatchet
- [ ] Whistle
- [ ] Bandana
- [ ] Quick-dry towels
- [ ] Waterproof bags
- [ ] Ziplock bags
- [ ] Trash bags
- [ ] Paper towels
- [ ] Bear can
- [ ] Binoculars
- [ ] Deck of cards/games
- [ ] Driver's license, registration, insurance, etc.
- [ ] Spare tire/jack
- [ ] Wiper blades
- [ ] Small amount of cash
- [ ] ....
- [ ] ....
- [ ] ....
- [ ] ....
- [ ] ....
- [ ] ....
- [ ] ....
- [ ] ....
- [ ] ....
- [ ] ....
- [ ] ....
- [ ] ....
- [ ] ....
- [ ] ....
- [ ] ....

PERSONALIZED LIST

- [ ] ....
- [ ] ....
- [ ] ....
- [ ] ....
- [ ] ....
- [ ] ....
- [ ] ....
- [ ] ....
- [ ] ....
- [ ] ....
- [ ] ....

TO BUY

- [ ] ....
- [ ] ....
- [ ] ....
- [ ] ....
- [ ] ....
- [ ] ....
- [ ] ....
- [ ] ....
- [ ] ....
- [ ] ....

ADDITIONAL NOTES

....
....
....
....
....
....
....
....
....
....
....
....
....
....

RECORD YOUR TRIP!

Park name: ....

State/territory: ....

Dates visited: ....

Nearby sites visited: ....

- 5 — Epic & life-changing experience
- 4 — Want to learn everything about this park!
- 3 — See why this place is so special
- 2 — Happy I went and had some good times
- 1 — Once and done!

FAVORITE CAMPSITE OR LODGING: ....

....

PEAK EXPERIENCE: ....

....

FAVORITE ADVENTURE: ....

....

FAVORITE LOCATION: ....

....

FAVORITE PHOTO: ....

....

BEST WILDLIFE SIGHTING: ....

....

FUN THING(S) I LEARNED ABOUT THE PARK: ....

....

INTERESTING PEOPLE MET ALONG MY JOURNEY: ....

....

VALUABLE RESOURCE(S) DISCOVERED ALONG THE WAY: ....

....

FOOD I COULDN'T LIVE WITHOUT: ....

....

THE BIGGEST CHALLENGE I FACED: ....

....

I WAS MOST PREPARED WHEN: ....

....

WISH I KNEW BEFORE I WENT: ....

....

WISH I WOULD HAVE BROUGHT: ....

....

MOST USEFUL PIECE OF GEAR: ....

....

MOST VALUABLE TOOL: ....

....

MOST USEFUL PIECE OF ADVICE: ....

....

TIPS FOR OTHER TRAVELERS: ....

....

ADDITIONAL NOTES: ....

....

....

....

PLAN YOUR TRIP!

Park name: ....

State/territory: .... Temperature range: ....

Planned dates: .... Altitude range: ....

Time zone: .... Latitude/longitude: ....

COMMITMENT LEVEL

- 6 — Full throttle, all-in adventure time!
- 5 — Bring on a big challenge!
- 4 — Many trails, sites, & adventures planned!
- 3 — Rolling where the wind blows me!
- 2 — Tons to do without breaking a big sweat!
- 1 — Easy-going, leisurely days...

SEASON OF VISIT

- ☐ Spring
- ☐ Summer
- ☐ Autumn
- ☐ Winter

TOURING/SUPPORT

- ☐ Self-guided
- ☐ Privately guided
- ☐ Chartered trip
- ☐ Group trip
- ☐ Volunteering
- ☐ Ranger-led tours
- ☐ Instructional classes
- ☐ Special events
- ....
- ....
- ....
- ....
- ....

PARK TRANSPORT

- ☐ Car
- ☐ Bus
- ☐ RV/travel trailer
- ☐ Boat
- ☐ Float plane/bush plane
- ☐ Helicopter
- ☐ Tour bus
- ☐ All-terrain vehicle
- ☐ ....

PARK ITEMS TO PICK UP

- ☐ NPS annual pass
- ☐ NPS parks passport
- ☐ Pins, patches, & stickers
- ☐ Hiking stick medallions
- ☐ NPS maps & literature
- ☐ ....
- ☐ ....
- ☐ ....

RESOURCES/CONTACTS

- ☐ NPS visitor center(s):
  ....
- ☐ Wilderness permit(s):
  ....
- ☐ Tour company:
  ....
- ☐ Local guide(s):
  ....
- ☐ Local gear outfitter(s):
  ....
- ☐ Emergency services:
  ....
- ☐ Miscellaneous contact:
  ....
- ☐ Miscellaneous contact:
  ....

MAIN ACCOMMODATIONS

- ☐ NPS lodge
- ☐ Hotel
- ☐ RV/travel trailer
- ☐ Tent camping
- ☐ Backcountry camping
- ☐ Staying with friends
- ☐ Houseboat
- ☐ Cruise ship
- ☐ Van/car
- ☐ ....
- ☐ ....

AMENITIES

- ☐ Campgrounds
  - ☐ Standard
  - ☐ RV
  - ☐ Primitive
  - ☐ Day use only
  - ☐ Group
- ☐ Plumbed bathrooms
- ☐ Showers
- ☐ Park store
- ☐ Wi-Fi
- ☐ NPS amphitheater
- ☐ Pet-friendly
- ☐ ....
- ☐ ....

IN-TOW

- ☐ Spouse/partner
- ☐ Children
- ☐ Pets
- ☐ Friends
- ☐ Extended family
- ☐ Boatloads of gear!
- ☐ ....
- ☐ ....

ADVANCED PLANNING

- ☐ Physical training?

  ....

  ....
- ☐ Seasonal aspects?

  ....

  ....
- ☐ Obtained permits?

  ....

  ....
- ☐ Purchased gear?

  ....

  ....

  ....

FINAL SAFETY CHECKS

- ☐ Left your trip plan with an emergency contact back home?
- ☐ Reviewed basic emergency aid procedures?
- ☐ Additional forms/permits needed?
- ☐ Checked on closures/mandates that might affect your travel?
- ☐ ....
- ☐ ....
- ☐ ....

MAIN GOALS

- ☐ Solitude
- ☐ Active adventure
- ☐ Creative pursuits
- ☐ Learning
- ☐ Endurance training
- ☐ Gathering loved ones
- ☐ Seeing new things!
- ☐ ....
- ☐ ....
- ☐ ....

IMMERSIVE EXPERIENCES

- ☐ Cultural/historical
- ☐ Volunteering
- ☐ Park programs
- ☐ Junior Ranger program
- ☐ NPS-guided night walks
- ☐ School/youth trips
- ☐ Teacher/educator programs
- ☐ Professional development
- ☐ ....
- ☐ ....
- ☐ ....

ADVENTURE GOALS

- ☐ Hiking big trails
- ☐ Easy day hikes
- ☐ Cycling/mountain biking/fat biking
- ☐ Kayaking/canoeing/SUP
- ☐ Trail running
- ☐ Rafting
- ☐ Swimming
- ☐ Backpacking
- ☐ Wildlife viewing
- ☐ Scenic drives
- ☐ Fishing/angling
- ☐ Mountaineering
- ☐ Climbing/bouldering
- ☐ Photography
- ☐ Birdwatching
- ☐ Stargazing
- ☐ Cultural immersion
- ☐ Endurance training
- ☐ Picnicking
- ☐ ....

PHOTOGRAPHY PLANS

- ☐ Wildlife
- ☐ Birds
- ☐ Landscapes
- ☐ Night skies
- ☐ People
- ☐ Cultural artifacts
- ☐ Macro/abstract
- ☐ Family pictures
- ☐ Selfies
- ☐ ....

ADDITIONAL NOTES

....

....

....

....

PACK FOR YOUR TRIP!

Park name: ....

HEALTH & PERSONAL ITEMS

- [ ] Premade first aid kit
- [ ] Wildlife/insect protection
- [ ] Medications
  - ....
  - ....
- [ ] Supplements
  - ....
  - ....
- [ ] Eyeglasses/contacts
- [ ] Sun/wind/snow protection (eyes/skin/face)
- [ ] Facial tissues
- [ ] Bug spray
- [ ] Antibacterial wipes
- [ ] ....
- [ ] ....

ELECTRONICS

- [ ] Camera
  - [ ] Tripod
  - [ ] Lenses/lens cloths
  - [ ] Memory cards
  - [ ] Batteries & charger
- [ ] Weather protection
- [ ] External charging device
- [ ] Phone & charging cord
- [ ] Mobile Wi-Fi device
- [ ] Electronic tablet
- [ ] Satellite phone
- [ ] Personal locater beacon
- [ ] ....

CLOTHING/SHOES

- [ ] Insulated jacket
- [ ] Rain jacket/pants
- [ ] Thermal layers
- [ ] Wicked/quick-dry clothing
- [ ] Loose-fitting shirts
- [ ] Loose-fitting pants
- [ ] Hiking pants/shorts
- [ ] Short-sleeved/sleeveless shirts
- [ ] Full winter gear
  - ....
  - ....
  - ....
- [ ] Leisurewear
- [ ] Beachwear
- [ ] Hiking shoes
- [ ] Athletic shoes
- [ ] Water shoes
- [ ] Sandals/flip-flops
- [ ] Neck gaiter
- [ ] Sun hat/cap
- [ ] Stocking cap
- [ ] Socks + extra pair
- [ ] Undergarments
- [ ] Gloves/mittens
- [ ] ....
- [ ] ....
- [ ] ....
- [ ] ....
- [ ] ....
- [ ] ....

OUTDOOR GEAR

- [ ] Hiking poles
- [ ] Tent
- [ ] Sleeping bag
- [ ] Sleeping pad
- [ ] Pillow
- [ ] Shade tent
- [ ] Emergency space blanket
- [ ] Tarp
- [ ] Daypack
- [ ] Headlamp(s)
- [ ] Lantern(s)
- [ ] Water filter & iodine tablets
- [ ] Large refillable water jug
- [ ] Portable stove
- [ ] Hot beverage thermos
- [ ] Nylon hammock
- [ ] Throw blanket
- [ ] Reusable dishes/cutlery
- [ ] Hand warmers
- [ ] ....
- [ ] ....
- [ ] ....
- [ ] ....
- [ ] ....
- [ ] ....
- [ ] ....
- [ ] ....
- [ ] ....
- [ ] ....

FOOD & DRINK

- [ ] Water
- [ ] Refillable water bottle
- [ ] Energy drinks with electrolytes
- [ ] Protein-packed snacks
- [ ] Salty, easy-to-digest snacks
- [ ] Dehydrated food
- [ ] No-cook food items
- [ ] ....
- [ ] ....
- [ ] ....
- [ ] ....
- [ ] ....
- [ ] ....
- [ ] ....
- [ ] ....
- [ ] ....
- [ ] ....
- [ ] ....
- [ ] ....
- [ ] ....
- [ ] ....

PARK-SPECIFIC

- [ ] *The National Parks Journal*!
- [ ] Permits
- [ ] Guidebooks
- [ ] Park map
- [ ] ....
- [ ] ....
- [ ] ....
- [ ] ....
- [ ] ....
- [ ] ....

MISCELLANEOUS

- [ ] Duct tape
- [ ] Multipurpose tool
- [ ] Knife
- [ ] Scissors
- [ ] Can opener
- [ ] Matches/lighter/ firestarter
- [ ] Hatchet
- [ ] Whistle
- [ ] Bandana
- [ ] Quick-dry towels
- [ ] Waterproof bags
- [ ] Ziplock bags
- [ ] Trash bags
- [ ] Paper towels
- [ ] Bear can
- [ ] Binoculars
- [ ] Deck of cards/games
- [ ] Driver's license, registration, insurance, etc.
- [ ] Spare tire/jack
- [ ] Wiper blades
- [ ] Small amount of cash
- [ ] ....
- [ ] ....
- [ ] ....
- [ ] ....
- [ ] ....
- [ ] ....
- [ ] ....
- [ ] ....
- [ ] ....
- [ ] ....
- [ ] ....
- [ ] ....
- [ ] ....
- [ ] ....

PERSONALIZED LIST

- [ ] ....
- [ ] ....
- [ ] ....
- [ ] ....
- [ ] ....
- [ ] ....
- [ ] ....
- [ ] ....
- [ ] ....
- [ ] ....

TO BUY

- [ ] ....
- [ ] ....
- [ ] ....
- [ ] ....
- [ ] ....
- [ ] ....
- [ ] ....
- [ ] ....
- [ ] ....
- [ ] ....

ADDITIONAL NOTES

....
....
....
....
....
....
....
....
....
....
....
....
....
....
....

RECORD YOUR TRIP!

Park name: ....

State/territory: ....

Dates visited: ....

Nearby sites visited: ....

ARROWHEAD RATING!

5 — Epic & life-changing experience
4 — Want to learn everything about this park!
3 — See why this place is so special
2 — Happy I went and had some good times
1 — Once and done!

FAVORITE CAMPSITE OR LODGING: ....
....

PEAK EXPERIENCE: ....
....

FAVORITE ADVENTURE: ....
....

FAVORITE LOCATION: ....
....

FAVORITE PHOTO: ....
....

BEST WILDLIFE SIGHTING: ....
....

FUN THING(S) I LEARNED ABOUT THE PARK: ....
....

INTERESTING PEOPLE MET ALONG MY JOURNEY: ....

....

VALUABLE RESOURCE(S) DISCOVERED ALONG THE WAY: ....

....

FOOD I COULDN'T LIVE WITHOUT: ....

....

THE BIGGEST CHALLENGE I FACED: ....

....

I WAS MOST PREPARED WHEN: ....

....

WISH I KNEW BEFORE I WENT: ....

....

WISH I WOULD HAVE BROUGHT: ....

....

MOST USEFUL PIECE OF GEAR: ....

....

MOST VALUABLE TOOL: ....

....

MOST USEFUL PIECE OF ADVICE: ....

....

TIPS FOR OTHER TRAVELERS: ....

....

ADDITIONAL NOTES: ....

....

....

....

....

PLAN YOUR TRIP!

Park name: ....

State/territory: ....   Temperature range: ....

Planned dates: ....   Altitude range: ....

Time zone: ....   Latitude/longitude: ....

COMMITMENT LEVEL

- 6 — Full throttle, all-in adventure time!
- 5 — Bring on a big challenge!
- 4 — Many trails, sites, & adventures planned!
- 3 — Rolling where the wind blows me!
- 2 — Tons to do without breaking a big sweat!
- 1 — Easy-going, leisurely days...

SEASON OF VISIT

- ☐ Spring
- ☐ Summer
- ☐ Autumn
- ☐ Winter

TOURING/SUPPORT

- ☐ Self-guided
- ☐ Privately guided
- ☐ Chartered trip
- ☐ Group trip
- ☐ Volunteering
- ☐ Ranger-led tours
- ☐ Instructional classes
- ☐ Special events
- ....
- ....
- ....
- ....
- ....

PARK TRANSPORT

- ☐ Car
- ☐ Bus
- ☐ RV/travel trailer
- ☐ Boat
- ☐ Float plane/bush plane
- ☐ Helicopter
- ☐ Tour bus
- ☐ All-terrain vehicle
- ☐ ....

PARK ITEMS TO PICK UP

- ☐ NPS annual pass
- ☐ NPS parks passport
- ☐ Pins, patches, & stickers
- ☐ Hiking stick medallions
- ☐ NPS maps & literature
- ☐ ....
- ☐ ....
- ☐ ....

RESOURCES/CONTACTS

- ☐ NPS visitor center(s): ....
- ☐ Wilderness permit(s): ....
- ☐ Tour company: ....
- ☐ Local guide(s): ....
- ☐ Local gear outfitter(s): ....
- ☐ Emergency services: ....
- ☐ Miscellaneous contact: ....
- ☐ Miscellaneous contact: ....

MAIN ACCOMMODATIONS

- ☐ NPS lodge
- ☐ Hotel
- ☐ RV/travel trailer
- ☐ Tent camping
- ☐ Backcountry camping
- ☐ Staying with friends
- ☐ Houseboat
- ☐ Cruise ship
- ☐ Van/car
- ☐ ....
- ☐ ....

AMENITIES

- [ ] Campgrounds
  - [ ] Standard
  - [ ] RV
  - [ ] Primitive
  - [ ] Day use only
  - [ ] Group
- [ ] Plumbed bathrooms
- [ ] Showers
- [ ] Park store
- [ ] Wi-Fi
- [ ] NPS amphitheater
- [ ] Pet-friendly
- [ ] ----------------------------------
- [ ] ----------------------------------

IN-TOW

- [ ] Spouse/partner
- [ ] Children
- [ ] Pets
- [ ] Friends
- [ ] Extended family
- [ ] Boatloads of gear!
- [ ] ----------------------------------
- [ ] ----------------------------------

ADVANCED PLANNING

- [ ] Physical training?

- [ ] Seasonal aspects?

- [ ] Obtained permits?

- [ ] Purchased gear?

FINAL SAFETY CHECKS

- [ ] Left your trip plan with an emergency contact back home?
- [ ] Reviewed basic emergency aid procedures?
- [ ] Additional forms/permits needed?
- [ ] Checked on closures/mandates that might affect your travel?
- [ ] ----------------------------------
- [ ] ----------------------------------
- [ ] ----------------------------------

MAIN GOALS

- [ ] Solitude
- [ ] Active adventure
- [ ] Creative pursuits
- [ ] Learning
- [ ] Endurance training
- [ ] Gathering loved ones
- [ ] Seeing new things!
- [ ] ----------------------------------
- [ ] ----------------------------------
- [ ] ----------------------------------

IMMERSIVE EXPERIENCES

- [ ] Cultural/historical
- [ ] Volunteering
- [ ] Park programs
- [ ] Junior Ranger program
- [ ] NPS-guided night walks
- [ ] School/youth trips
- [ ] Teacher/educator programs
- [ ] Professional development
- [ ] ----------------------------------
- [ ] ----------------------------------
- [ ] ----------------------------------

ADVENTURE GOALS

- [ ] Hiking big trails
- [ ] Easy day hikes
- [ ] Cycling/mountain biking/fat biking
- [ ] Kayaking/canoeing/SUP
- [ ] Trail running
- [ ] Rafting
- [ ] Swimming
- [ ] Backpacking
- [ ] Wildlife viewing
- [ ] Scenic drives
- [ ] Fishing/angling
- [ ] Mountaineering
- [ ] Climbing/bouldering
- [ ] Photography
- [ ] Birdwatching
- [ ] Stargazing
- [ ] Cultural immersion
- [ ] Endurance training
- [ ] Picnicking
- [ ] ----------------------------------

PHOTOGRAPHY PLANS

- [ ] Wildlife
- [ ] Birds
- [ ] Landscapes
- [ ] Night skies
- [ ] People
- [ ] Cultural artifacts
- [ ] Macro/abstract
- [ ] Family pictures
- [ ] Selfies
- [ ] ----------------------------------

ADDITIONAL NOTES

PACK FOR YOUR TRIP!

Park name: ....

HEALTH & PERSONAL ITEMS

- [ ] Premade first aid kit
- [ ] Wildlife/insect protection
- [ ] Medications
  - ....
  - ....
- [ ] Supplements
  - ....
  - ....
- [ ] Eyeglasses/contacts
- [ ] Sun/wind/snow protection (eyes/skin/face)
- [ ] Facial tissues
- [ ] Bug spray
- [ ] Antibacterial wipes
- [ ] ....
- [ ] ....

ELECTRONICS

- [ ] Camera
  - [ ] Tripod
  - [ ] Lenses/lens cloths
  - [ ] Memory cards
  - [ ] Batteries & charger
- [ ] Weather protection
- [ ] External charging device
- [ ] Phone & charging cord
- [ ] Mobile Wi-Fi device
- [ ] Electronic tablet
- [ ] Satellite phone
- [ ] Personal locater beacon
- [ ] ....

CLOTHING/SHOES

- [ ] Insulated jacket
- [ ] Rain jacket/pants
- [ ] Thermal layers
- [ ] Wicked/quick-dry clothing
- [ ] Loose-fitting shirts
- [ ] Loose-fitting pants
- [ ] Hiking pants/shorts
- [ ] Short-sleeved/sleeveless shirts
- [ ] Full winter gear
  - ....
  - ....
  - ....
- [ ] Leisurewear
- [ ] Beachwear
- [ ] Hiking shoes
- [ ] Athletic shoes
- [ ] Water shoes
- [ ] Sandals/flip-flops
- [ ] Neck gaiter
- [ ] Sun hat/cap
- [ ] Stocking cap
- [ ] Socks + extra pair
- [ ] Undergarments
- [ ] Gloves/mittens
- [ ] ....
- [ ] ....
- [ ] ....
- [ ] ....
- [ ] ....

OUTDOOR GEAR

- [ ] Hiking poles
- [ ] Tent
- [ ] Sleeping bag
- [ ] Sleeping pad
- [ ] Pillow
- [ ] Shade tent
- [ ] Emergency space blanket
- [ ] Tarp
- [ ] Daypack
- [ ] Headlamp(s)
- [ ] Lantern(s)
- [ ] Water filter & iodine tablets
- [ ] Large refillable water jug
- [ ] Portable stove
- [ ] Hot beverage thermos
- [ ] Nylon hammock
- [ ] Throw blanket
- [ ] Reusable dishes/cutlery
- [ ] Hand warmers
- [ ] ....
- [ ] ....
- [ ] ....
- [ ] ....
- [ ] ....
- [ ] ....
- [ ] ....
- [ ] ....
- [ ] ....

FOOD & DRINK

- [ ] Water
- [ ] Refillable water bottle
- [ ] Energy drinks with electrolytes
- [ ] Protein-packed snacks
- [ ] Salty, easy-to-digest snacks
- [ ] Dehydrated food
- [ ] No-cook food items
- [ ] ....
- [ ] ....
- [ ] ....
- [ ] ....
- [ ] ....
- [ ] ....
- [ ] ....
- [ ] ....
- [ ] ....
- [ ] ....
- [ ] ....
- [ ] ....
- [ ] ....
- [ ] ....
- [ ] ....

PARK-SPECIFIC

- [ ] *The National Parks Journal*!
- [ ] Permits
- [ ] Guidebooks
- [ ] Park map
- [ ] ....
- [ ] ....
- [ ] ....
- [ ] ....
- [ ] ....
- [ ] ....

MISCELLANEOUS

- [ ] Duct tape
- [ ] Multipurpose tool
- [ ] Knife
- [ ] Scissors
- [ ] Can opener
- [ ] Matches/lighter/ firestarter
- [ ] Hatchet
- [ ] Whistle
- [ ] Bandana
- [ ] Quick-dry towels
- [ ] Waterproof bags
- [ ] Ziplock bags
- [ ] Trash bags
- [ ] Paper towels
- [ ] Bear can
- [ ] Binoculars
- [ ] Deck of cards/games
- [ ] Driver's license, registration, insurance, etc.
- [ ] Spare tire/jack
- [ ] Wiper blades
- [ ] Small amount of cash
- [ ] ....
- [ ] ....
- [ ] ....
- [ ] ....
- [ ] ....
- [ ] ....
- [ ] ....
- [ ] ....
- [ ] ....
- [ ] ....
- [ ] ....
- [ ] ....
- [ ] ....
- [ ] ....
- [ ] ....

PERSONALIZED LIST

- [ ] ....
- [ ] ....
- [ ] ....
- [ ] ....
- [ ] ....
- [ ] ....
- [ ] ....
- [ ] ....
- [ ] ....
- [ ] ....

TO BUY

- [ ] ....
- [ ] ....
- [ ] ....
- [ ] ....
- [ ] ....
- [ ] ....
- [ ] ....
- [ ] ....
- [ ] ....

ADDITIONAL NOTES

....
....
....
....
....
....
....
....
....
....
....
....
....
....
....

RECORD YOUR TRIP!

Park name: ....

State/territory: ....

Dates visited: ....

Nearby sites visited: ....

ARROWHEAD RATING!

5 — Epic & life-changing experience

4 — Want to learn everything about this park!

3 — See why this place is so special

2 — Happy I went and had some good times

1 — Once and done!

FAVORITE CAMPSITE OR LODGING: ....

....

PEAK EXPERIENCE: ....

....

FAVORITE ADVENTURE: ....

....

FAVORITE LOCATION: ....

....

FAVORITE PHOTO: ....

....

BEST WILDLIFE SIGHTING: ....

....

FUN THING(S) I LEARNED ABOUT THE PARK: ....

....

INTERESTING PEOPLE MET ALONG MY JOURNEY: ....

....

VALUABLE RESOURCE(S) DISCOVERED ALONG THE WAY: ....

....

FOOD I COULDN'T LIVE WITHOUT: ....

....

THE BIGGEST CHALLENGE I FACED: ....

....

I WAS MOST PREPARED WHEN: ....

....

WISH I KNEW BEFORE I WENT: ....

....

WISH I WOULD HAVE BROUGHT: ....

....

MOST USEFUL PIECE OF GEAR: ....

....

MOST VALUABLE TOOL: ....

....

MOST USEFUL PIECE OF ADVICE: ....

....

TIPS FOR OTHER TRAVELERS: ....

....

ADDITIONAL NOTES: ....

....

....

....

....

PLAN YOUR TRIP!

Park name: ....

State/territory: ....

Planned dates: ....

Time zone: ....

Temperature range: ....

Altitude range: ....

Latitude/longitude: ....

COMMITMENT LEVEL

6 — Full throttle, all-in adventure time!

5 — Bring on a big challenge!

4 — Many trails, sites, & adventures planned!

3 — Rolling where the wind blows me!

2 — Tons to do without breaking a big sweat!

1 — Easy-going, leisurely days...

SEASON OF VISIT

☐ Spring
☐ Summer
☐ Autumn
☐ Winter

TOURING/SUPPORT

☐ Self-guided
☐ Privately guided
☐ Chartered trip
☐ Group trip
☐ Volunteering
☐ Ranger-led tours
☐ Instructional classes
☐ Special events
☐ ....
☐ ....
☐ ....
☐ ....
☐ ....

PARK TRANSPORT

☐ Car
☐ Bus
☐ RV/travel trailer
☐ Boat
☐ Float plane/bush plane
☐ Helicopter
☐ Tour bus
☐ All-terrain vehicle
☐ ....

PARK ITEMS TO PICK UP

☐ NPS annual pass
☐ NPS parks passport
☐ Pins, patches, & stickers
☐ Hiking stick medallions
☐ NPS maps & literature
☐ ....
☐ ....
☐ ....

RESOURCES/CONTACTS

☐ NPS visitor center(s):
....
☐ Wilderness permit(s):
....
☐ Tour company:
....
☐ Local guide(s):
....
☐ Local gear outfitter(s):
....
☐ Emergency services:
....
☐ Miscellaneous contact:
....
☐ Miscellaneous contact:
....

MAIN ACCOMMODATIONS

☐ NPS lodge
☐ Hotel
☐ RV/travel trailer
☐ Tent camping
☐ Backcountry camping
☐ Staying with friends
☐ Houseboat
☐ Cruise ship
☐ Van/car
☐ ....
☐ ....

AMENITIES

- [ ] Campgrounds
  - [ ] Standard
  - [ ] RV
  - [ ] Primitive
  - [ ] Day use only
  - [ ] Group
- [ ] Plumbed bathrooms
- [ ] Showers
- [ ] Park store
- [ ] Wi-Fi
- [ ] NPS amphitheater
- [ ] Pet-friendly
- [ ] ....
- [ ] ....

IN-TOW

- [ ] Spouse/partner
- [ ] Children
- [ ] Pets
- [ ] Friends
- [ ] Extended family
- [ ] Boatloads of gear!
- [ ] ....
- [ ] ....

ADVANCED PLANNING

- [ ] Physical training?

....

....

- [ ] Seasonal aspects?

....

....

- [ ] Obtained permits?

....

....

- [ ] Purchased gear?

....

....

....

FINAL SAFETY CHECKS

- [ ] Left your trip plan with an emergency contact back home?
- [ ] Reviewed basic emergency aid procedures?
- [ ] Additional forms/permits needed?
- [ ] Checked on closures/mandates that might affect your travel?
- [ ] ....
- [ ] ....
- [ ] ....

MAIN GOALS

- [ ] Solitude
- [ ] Active adventure
- [ ] Creative pursuits
- [ ] Learning
- [ ] Endurance training
- [ ] Gathering loved ones
- [ ] Seeing new things!
- [ ] ....
- [ ] ....
- [ ] ....

IMMERSIVE EXPERIENCES

- [ ] Cultural/historical
- [ ] Volunteering
- [ ] Park programs
- [ ] Junior Ranger program
- [ ] NPS-guided night walks
- [ ] School/youth trips
- [ ] Teacher/educator programs
- [ ] Professional development
- [ ] ....
- [ ] ....
- [ ] ....

ADVENTURE GOALS

- [ ] Hiking big trails
- [ ] Easy day hikes
- [ ] Cycling/mountain biking/fat biking
- [ ] Kayaking/canoeing/SUP
- [ ] Trail running
- [ ] Rafting
- [ ] Swimming
- [ ] Backpacking
- [ ] Wildlife viewing
- [ ] Scenic drives
- [ ] Fishing/angling
- [ ] Mountaineering
- [ ] Climbing/bouldering
- [ ] Photography
- [ ] Birdwatching
- [ ] Stargazing
- [ ] Cultural immersion
- [ ] Endurance training
- [ ] Picnicking
- [ ] ....

PHOTOGRAPHY PLANS

- [ ] Wildlife
- [ ] Birds
- [ ] Landscapes
- [ ] Night skies
- [ ] People
- [ ] Cultural artifacts
- [ ] Macro/abstract
- [ ] Family pictures
- [ ] Selfies
- [ ] ....

ADDITIONAL NOTES

....

....

....

....

PACK FOR YOUR TRIP!

Park name: ....

HEALTH & PERSONAL ITEMS

- [ ] Premade first aid kit
- [ ] Wildlife/insect protection
- [ ] Medications
- [ ] ....
- [ ] ....
- [ ] Supplements
- [ ] ....
- [ ] ....
- [ ] Eyeglasses/contacts
- [ ] Sun/wind/snow protection (eyes/skin/face)
- [ ] Facial tissues
- [ ] Bug spray
- [ ] Antibacterial wipes
- [ ] ....
- [ ] ....

ELECTRONICS

- [ ] Camera
  - [ ] Tripod
  - [ ] Lenses/lens cloths
  - [ ] Memory cards
  - [ ] Batteries & charger
- [ ] Weather protection
- [ ] External charging device
- [ ] Phone & charging cord
- [ ] Mobile Wi-Fi device
- [ ] Electronic tablet
- [ ] Satellite phone
- [ ] Personal locater beacon
- [ ] ....

CLOTHING/SHOES

- [ ] Insulated jacket
- [ ] Rain jacket/pants
- [ ] Thermal layers
- [ ] Wicked/quick-dry clothing
- [ ] Loose-fitting shirts
- [ ] Loose-fitting pants
- [ ] Hiking pants/shorts
- [ ] Short-sleeved/sleeveless shirts
- [ ] Full winter gear
- [ ] ....
- [ ] ....
- [ ] ....
- [ ] Leisurewear
- [ ] Beachwear
- [ ] Hiking shoes
- [ ] Athletic shoes
- [ ] Water shoes
- [ ] Sandals/flip-flops
- [ ] Neck gaiter
- [ ] Sun hat/cap
- [ ] Stocking cap
- [ ] Socks + extra pair
- [ ] Undergarments
- [ ] Gloves/mittens
- [ ] ....
- [ ] ....
- [ ] ....
- [ ] ....
- [ ] ....
- [ ] ....
- [ ] ....
- [ ] ....

OUTDOOR GEAR

- [ ] Hiking poles
- [ ] Tent
- [ ] Sleeping bag
- [ ] Sleeping pad
- [ ] Pillow
- [ ] Shade tent
- [ ] Emergency space blanket
- [ ] Tarp
- [ ] Daypack
- [ ] Headlamp(s)
- [ ] Lantern(s)
- [ ] Water filter & iodine tablets
- [ ] Large refillable water jug
- [ ] Portable stove
- [ ] Hot beverage thermos
- [ ] Nylon hammock
- [ ] Throw blanket
- [ ] Reusable dishes/cutlery
- [ ] Hand warmers
- [ ] ....
- [ ] ....
- [ ] ....
- [ ] ....
- [ ] ....
- [ ] ....
- [ ] ....
- [ ] ....
- [ ] ....
- [ ] ....

FOOD & DRINK

- [ ] Water
- [ ] Refillable water bottle
- [ ] Energy drinks with electrolytes
- [ ] Protein-packed snacks
- [ ] Salty, easy-to-digest snacks
- [ ] Dehydrated food
- [ ] No-cook food items
- [ ] ---
- [ ] ---
- [ ] ---
- [ ] ---
- [ ] ---
- [ ] ---
- [ ] ---
- [ ] ---
- [ ] ---
- [ ] ---
- [ ] ---
- [ ] ---
- [ ] ---
- [ ] ---

PARK-SPECIFIC

- [ ] *The National Parks Journal*!
- [ ] Permits
- [ ] Guidebooks
- [ ] Park map
- [ ] ---
- [ ] ---
- [ ] ---
- [ ] ---
- [ ] ---
- [ ] ---

MISCELLANEOUS

- [ ] Duct tape
- [ ] Multipurpose tool
- [ ] Knife
- [ ] Scissors
- [ ] Can opener
- [ ] Matches/lighter/ firestarter
- [ ] Hatchet
- [ ] Whistle
- [ ] Bandana
- [ ] Quick-dry towels
- [ ] Waterproof bags
- [ ] Ziplock bags
- [ ] Trash bags
- [ ] Paper towels
- [ ] Bear can
- [ ] Binoculars
- [ ] Deck of cards/games
- [ ] Driver's license, registration, insurance, etc.
- [ ] Spare tire/jack
- [ ] Wiper blades
- [ ] Small amount of cash
- [ ] ---
- [ ] ---
- [ ] ---
- [ ] ---
- [ ] ---
- [ ] ---
- [ ] ---
- [ ] ---
- [ ] ---
- [ ] ---
- [ ] ---
- [ ] ---
- [ ] ---

PERSONALIZED LIST

- [ ] ---
- [ ] ---
- [ ] ---
- [ ] ---
- [ ] ---
- [ ] ---
- [ ] ---
- [ ] ---
- [ ] ---
- [ ] ---

TO BUY

- [ ] ---
- [ ] ---
- [ ] ---
- [ ] ---
- [ ] ---
- [ ] ---
- [ ] ---
- [ ] ---
- [ ] ---
- [ ] ---

ADDITIONAL NOTES

RECORD YOUR TRIP!

Park name: ....

State/territory: ....

Dates visited: ....

Nearby sites visited: ....

ARROWHEAD RATING!

5 — Epic & life-changing experience

4 — Want to learn everything about this park!

3 — See why this place is so special

2 — Happy I went and had some good times

1 — Once and done!

FAVORITE CAMPSITE OR LODGING: ....
....

PEAK EXPERIENCE: ....
....

FAVORITE ADVENTURE: ....
....

FAVORITE LOCATION: ....
....

FAVORITE PHOTO: ....
....

BEST WILDLIFE SIGHTING: ....
....

FUN THING(S) I LEARNED ABOUT THE PARK: ....
....

INTERESTING PEOPLE MET ALONG MY JOURNEY: --

VALUABLE RESOURCE(S) DISCOVERED ALONG THE WAY: ---

FOOD I COULDN'T LIVE WITHOUT: --

THE BIGGEST CHALLENGE I FACED: --

I WAS MOST PREPARED WHEN: ---

WISH I KNEW BEFORE I WENT: ---

WISH I WOULD HAVE BROUGHT: --

MOST USEFUL PIECE OF GEAR: ---

MOST VALUABLE TOOL: --

MOST USEFUL PIECE OF ADVICE: --

TIPS FOR OTHER TRAVELERS: --

ADDITIONAL NOTES: ---

PLAN YOUR TRIP!

Park name: ....

State/territory: .... Temperature range: ....

Planned dates: .... Altitude range: ....

Time zone: .... Latitude/longitude: ....

COMMITMENT LEVEL

6 — Full throttle, all-in adventure time!

5 — Bring on a big challenge!

4 — Many trails, sites, & adventures planned!

3 — Rolling where the wind blows me!

2 — Tons to do without breaking a big sweat!

1 — Easy-going, leisurely days...

SEASON OF VISIT

- [ ] Spring
- [ ] Summer
- [ ] Autumn
- [ ] Winter

TOURING/SUPPORT

- [ ] Self-guided
- [ ] Privately guided
- [ ] Chartered trip
- [ ] Group trip
- [ ] Volunteering
- [ ] Ranger-led tours
- [ ] Instructional classes
- [ ] Special events
- ....
- ....
- ....
- ....
- ....

PARK TRANSPORT

- [ ] Car
- [ ] Bus
- [ ] RV/travel trailer
- [ ] Boat
- [ ] Float plane/bush plane
- [ ] Helicopter
- [ ] Tour bus
- [ ] All-terrain vehicle
- [ ] ....

PARK ITEMS TO PICK UP

- [ ] NPS annual pass
- [ ] NPS parks passport
- [ ] Pins, patches, & stickers
- [ ] Hiking stick medallions
- [ ] NPS maps & literature
- [ ] ....
- [ ] ....
- [ ] ....

RESOURCES/CONTACTS

- [ ] NPS visitor center(s):
  ....
- [ ] Wilderness permit(s):
  ....
- [ ] Tour company:
  ....
- [ ] Local guide(s):
  ....
- [ ] Local gear outfitter(s):
  ....
- [ ] Emergency services:
  ....
- [ ] Miscellaneous contact:
  ....
- [ ] Miscellaneous contact:
  ....

MAIN ACCOMMODATIONS

- [ ] NPS lodge
- [ ] Hotel
- [ ] RV/travel trailer
- [ ] Tent camping
- [ ] Backcountry camping
- [ ] Staying with friends
- [ ] Houseboat
- [ ] Cruise ship
- [ ] Van/car
- [ ] ....
- [ ] ....

AMENITIES

- [ ] Campgrounds
  - [ ] Standard
  - [ ] RV
  - [ ] Primitive
  - [ ] Day use only
  - [ ] Group
- [ ] Plumbed bathrooms
- [ ] Showers
- [ ] Park store
- [ ] Wi-Fi
- [ ] NPS amphitheater
- [ ] Pet-friendly
- [ ] --------------------------------
- [ ] --------------------------------

IN-TOW

- [ ] Spouse/partner
- [ ] Children
- [ ] Pets
- [ ] Friends
- [ ] Extended family
- [ ] Boatloads of gear!
- [ ] --------------------------------
- [ ] --------------------------------

ADVANCED PLANNING

- [ ] Physical training?

- [ ] Seasonal aspects?

- [ ] Obtained permits?

- [ ] Purchased gear?

FINAL SAFETY CHECKS

- [ ] Left your trip plan with an emergency contact back home?
- [ ] Reviewed basic emergency aid procedures?
- [ ] Additional forms/permits needed?
- [ ] Checked on closures/mandates that might affect your travel?
- [ ] --------------------------------
- [ ] --------------------------------
- [ ] --------------------------------

MAIN GOALS

- [ ] Solitude
- [ ] Active adventure
- [ ] Creative pursuits
- [ ] Learning
- [ ] Endurance training
- [ ] Gathering loved ones
- [ ] Seeing new things!
- [ ] --------------------------------
- [ ] --------------------------------
- [ ] --------------------------------

IMMERSIVE EXPERIENCES

- [ ] Cultural/historical
- [ ] Volunteering
- [ ] Park programs
- [ ] Junior Ranger program
- [ ] NPS-guided night walks
- [ ] School/youth trips
- [ ] Teacher/educator programs
- [ ] Professional development
- [ ] --------------------------------
- [ ] --------------------------------
- [ ] --------------------------------

ADVENTURE GOALS

- [ ] Hiking big trails
- [ ] Easy day hikes
- [ ] Cycling/mountain biking/fat biking
- [ ] Kayaking/canoeing/SUP
- [ ] Trail running
- [ ] Rafting
- [ ] Swimming
- [ ] Backpacking
- [ ] Wildlife viewing
- [ ] Scenic drives
- [ ] Fishing/angling
- [ ] Mountaineering
- [ ] Climbing/bouldering
- [ ] Photography
- [ ] Birdwatching
- [ ] Stargazing
- [ ] Cultural immersion
- [ ] Endurance training
- [ ] Picnicking
- [ ] --------------------------------

PHOTOGRAPHY PLANS

- [ ] Wildlife
- [ ] Birds
- [ ] Landscapes
- [ ] Night skies
- [ ] People
- [ ] Cultural artifacts
- [ ] Macro/abstract
- [ ] Family pictures
- [ ] Selfies
- [ ] --------------------------------

ADDITIONAL NOTES

PACK FOR YOUR TRIP!

Park name: ....

HEALTH & PERSONAL ITEMS

- [ ] Premade first aid kit
- [ ] Wildlife/insect protection
- [ ] Medications
- [ ] ....
- [ ] ....
- [ ] Supplements
- [ ] ....
- [ ] ....
- [ ] Eyeglasses/contacts
- [ ] Sun/wind/snow protection (eyes/skin/face)
- [ ] Facial tissues
- [ ] Bug spray
- [ ] Antibacterial wipes
- [ ] ....
- [ ] ....

ELECTRONICS

- [ ] Camera
  - [ ] Tripod
  - [ ] Lenses/lens cloths
  - [ ] Memory cards
  - [ ] Batteries & charger
- [ ] Weather protection
- [ ] External charging device
- [ ] Phone & charging cord
- [ ] Mobile Wi-Fi device
- [ ] Electronic tablet
- [ ] Satellite phone
- [ ] Personal locater beacon
- [ ] ....

CLOTHING/SHOES

- [ ] Insulated jacket
- [ ] Rain jacket/pants
- [ ] Thermal layers
- [ ] Wicked/quick-dry clothing
- [ ] Loose-fitting shirts
- [ ] Loose-fitting pants
- [ ] Hiking pants/shorts
- [ ] Short-sleeved/sleeveless shirts
- [ ] Full winter gear
- [ ] ....
- [ ] ....
- [ ] ....
- [ ] Leisurewear
- [ ] Beachwear
- [ ] Hiking shoes
- [ ] Athletic shoes
- [ ] Water shoes
- [ ] Sandals/flip-flops
- [ ] Neck gaiter
- [ ] Sun hat/cap
- [ ] Stocking cap
- [ ] Socks + extra pair
- [ ] Undergarments
- [ ] Gloves/mittens
- [ ] ....
- [ ] ....
- [ ] ....
- [ ] ....
- [ ] ....
- [ ] ....

OUTDOOR GEAR

- [ ] Hiking poles
- [ ] Tent
- [ ] Sleeping bag
- [ ] Sleeping pad
- [ ] Pillow
- [ ] Shade tent
- [ ] Emergency space blanket
- [ ] Tarp
- [ ] Daypack
- [ ] Headlamp(s)
- [ ] Lantern(s)
- [ ] Water filter & iodine tablets
- [ ] Large refillable water jug
- [ ] Portable stove
- [ ] Hot beverage thermos
- [ ] Nylon hammock
- [ ] Throw blanket
- [ ] Reusable dishes/cutlery
- [ ] Hand warmers
- [ ] ....
- [ ] ....
- [ ] ....
- [ ] ....
- [ ] ....
- [ ] ....
- [ ] ....
- [ ] ....

FOOD & DRINK

- ☐ Water
- ☐ Refillable water bottle
- ☐ Energy drinks with electrolytes
- ☐ Protein-packed snacks
- ☐ Salty, easy-to-digest snacks
- ☐ Dehydrated food
- ☐ No-cook food items
- ☐ ....
- ☐ ....
- ☐ ....
- ☐ ....
- ☐ ....
- ☐ ....
- ☐ ....
- ☐ ....
- ☐ ....
- ☐ ....
- ☐ ....
- ☐ ....
- ☐ ....
- ☐ ....

PARK-SPECIFIC

- ☐ *The National Parks Journal*!
- ☐ Permits
- ☐ Guidebooks
- ☐ Park map
- ☐ ....
- ☐ ....
- ☐ ....
- ☐ ....
- ☐ ....
- ☐ ....

MISCELLANEOUS

- ☐ Duct tape
- ☐ Multipurpose tool
- ☐ Knife
- ☐ Scissors
- ☐ Can opener
- ☐ Matches/lighter/ firestarter
- ☐ Hatchet
- ☐ Whistle
- ☐ Bandana
- ☐ Quick-dry towels
- ☐ Waterproof bags
- ☐ Ziplock bags
- ☐ Trash bags
- ☐ Paper towels
- ☐ Bear can
- ☐ Binoculars
- ☐ Deck of cards/games
- ☐ Driver's license, registration, insurance, etc.
- ☐ Spare tire/jack
- ☐ Wiper blades
- ☐ Small amount of cash
- ☐ ....
- ☐ ....
- ☐ ....
- ☐ ....
- ☐ ....
- ☐ ....
- ☐ ....
- ☐ ....
- ☐ ....
- ☐ ....
- ☐ ....
- ☐ ....
- ☐ ....
- ☐ ....

PERSONALIZED LIST

- ☐ ....
- ☐ ....
- ☐ ....
- ☐ ....
- ☐ ....
- ☐ ....
- ☐ ....
- ☐ ....
- ☐ ....
- ☐ ....

TO BUY

- ☐ ....
- ☐ ....
- ☐ ....
- ☐ ....
- ☐ ....
- ☐ ....
- ☐ ....
- ☐ ....
- ☐ ....
- ☐ ....

ADDITIONAL NOTES

....
....
....
....
....
....
....
....
....
....
....
....
....
....

RECORD YOUR TRIP!

Park name: --

State/territory: --

Dates visited: --

Nearby sites visited: ---

ARROWHEAD RATING!

- 5 — Epic & life-changing experience
- 4 — Want to learn everything about this park!
- 3 — See why this place is so special
- 2 — Happy I went and had some good times
- 1 — Once and done!

FAVORITE CAMPSITE OR LODGING: --

PEAK EXPERIENCE: --

FAVORITE ADVENTURE: ---

FAVORITE LOCATION: --

FAVORITE PHOTO: ---

BEST WILDLIFE SIGHTING: ---

FUN THING(S) I LEARNED ABOUT THE PARK: --------------------------------------

----

INTERESTING PEOPLE MET ALONG MY JOURNEY: --

VALUABLE RESOURCE(S) DISCOVERED ALONG THE WAY: -----------------------------

----

FOOD I COULDN'T LIVE WITHOUT: --

THE BIGGEST CHALLENGE I FACED: ---

I WAS MOST PREPARED WHEN: --

WISH I KNEW BEFORE I WENT: ---

WISH I WOULD HAVE BROUGHT: ---

MOST USEFUL PIECE OF GEAR: ---

MOST VALUABLE TOOL: --

MOST USEFUL PIECE OF ADVICE: ---

TIPS FOR OTHER TRAVELERS: --

ADDITIONAL NOTES: --

PLAN YOUR TRIP!

Park name: ....

State/territory: ....   Temperature range: ....

Planned dates: ....   Altitude range: ....

Time zone: ....   Latitude/longitude: ....

COMMITMENT LEVEL

- 6 — Full throttle, all-in adventure time!
- 5 — Bring on a big challenge!
- 4 — Many trails, sites, & adventures planned!
- 3 — Rolling where the wind blows me!
- 2 — Tons to do without breaking a big sweat!
- 1 — Easy-going, leisurely days...

SEASON OF VISIT

- ☐ Spring
- ☐ Summer
- ☐ Autumn
- ☐ Winter

TOURING/SUPPORT

- ☐ Self-guided
- ☐ Privately guided
- ☐ Chartered trip
- ☐ Group trip
- ☐ Volunteering
- ☐ Ranger-led tours
- ☐ Instructional classes
- ☐ Special events
- ....
- ....
- ....
- ....
- ....

PARK TRANSPORT

- ☐ Car
- ☐ Bus
- ☐ RV/travel trailer
- ☐ Boat
- ☐ Float plane/bush plane
- ☐ Helicopter
- ☐ Tour bus
- ☐ All-terrain vehicle
- ☐ ....

PARK ITEMS TO PICK UP

- ☐ NPS annual pass
- ☐ NPS parks passport
- ☐ Pins, patches, & stickers
- ☐ Hiking stick medallions
- ☐ NPS maps & literature
- ☐ ....
- ☐ ....
- ☐ ....

RESOURCES/CONTACTS

- ☐ NPS visitor center(s):
- ☐ Wilderness permit(s):
- ☐ Tour company:
- ☐ Local guide(s):
- ☐ Local gear outfitter(s):
- ☐ Emergency services:
- ☐ Miscellaneous contact:
- ☐ Miscellaneous contact:

MAIN ACCOMMODATIONS

- ☐ NPS lodge
- ☐ Hotel
- ☐ RV/travel trailer
- ☐ Tent camping
- ☐ Backcountry camping
- ☐ Staying with friends
- ☐ Houseboat
- ☐ Cruise ship
- ☐ Van/car
- ☐ ....
- ☐ ....

AMENITIES

- [ ] Campgrounds
  - [ ] Standard
  - [ ] RV
  - [ ] Primitive
  - [ ] Day use only
  - [ ] Group
- [ ] Plumbed bathrooms
- [ ] Showers
- [ ] Park store
- [ ] Wi-Fi
- [ ] NPS amphitheater
- [ ] Pet-friendly
- [ ] ----------------------------
- [ ] ----------------------------

IN-TOW

- [ ] Spouse/partner
- [ ] Children
- [ ] Pets
- [ ] Friends
- [ ] Extended family
- [ ] Boatloads of gear!
- [ ] ----------------------------
- [ ] ----------------------------

ADVANCED PLANNING

- [ ] Physical training?

- [ ] Seasonal aspects?

- [ ] Obtained permits?

- [ ] Purchased gear?

FINAL SAFETY CHECKS

- [ ] Left your trip plan with an emergency contact back home?
- [ ] Reviewed basic emergency aid procedures?
- [ ] Additional forms/permits needed?
- [ ] Checked on closures/mandates that might affect your travel?
- [ ] ----------------------------
- [ ] ----------------------------
- [ ] ----------------------------

MAIN GOALS

- [ ] Solitude
- [ ] Active adventure
- [ ] Creative pursuits
- [ ] Learning
- [ ] Endurance training
- [ ] Gathering loved ones
- [ ] Seeing new things!
- [ ] ----------------------------
- [ ] ----------------------------
- [ ] ----------------------------

IMMERSIVE EXPERIENCES

- [ ] Cultural/historical
- [ ] Volunteering
- [ ] Park programs
- [ ] Junior Ranger program
- [ ] NPS-guided night walks
- [ ] School/youth trips
- [ ] Teacher/educator programs
- [ ] Professional development
- [ ] ----------------------------
- [ ] ----------------------------
- [ ] ----------------------------

ADVENTURE GOALS

- [ ] Hiking big trails
- [ ] Easy day hikes
- [ ] Cycling/mountain biking/fat biking
- [ ] Kayaking/canoeing/SUP
- [ ] Trail running
- [ ] Rafting
- [ ] Swimming
- [ ] Backpacking
- [ ] Wildlife viewing
- [ ] Scenic drives
- [ ] Fishing/angling
- [ ] Mountaineering
- [ ] Climbing/bouldering
- [ ] Photography
- [ ] Birdwatching
- [ ] Stargazing
- [ ] Cultural immersion
- [ ] Endurance training
- [ ] Picnicking
- [ ] ----------------------------

PHOTOGRAPHY PLANS

- [ ] Wildlife
- [ ] Birds
- [ ] Landscapes
- [ ] Night skies
- [ ] People
- [ ] Cultural artifacts
- [ ] Macro/abstract
- [ ] Family pictures
- [ ] Selfies
- [ ] ----------------------------

ADDITIONAL NOTES

PACK FOR YOUR TRIP!

Park name: ....

HEALTH & PERSONAL ITEMS

- [ ] Premade first aid kit
- [ ] Wildlife/insect protection
- [ ] Medications
- [ ] ....
- [ ] ....
- [ ] Supplements
- [ ] ....
- [ ] ....
- [ ] Eyeglasses/contacts
- [ ] Sun/wind/snow protection (eyes/skin/face)
- [ ] Facial tissues
- [ ] Bug spray
- [ ] Antibacterial wipes
- [ ] ....
- [ ] ....

ELECTRONICS

- [ ] Camera
  - [ ] Tripod
  - [ ] Lenses/lens cloths
  - [ ] Memory cards
  - [ ] Batteries & charger
- [ ] Weather protection
- [ ] External charging device
- [ ] Phone & charging cord
- [ ] Mobile Wi-Fi device
- [ ] Electronic tablet
- [ ] Satellite phone
- [ ] Personal locater beacon
- [ ] ....

CLOTHING/SHOES

- [ ] Insulated jacket
- [ ] Rain jacket/pants
- [ ] Thermal layers
- [ ] Wicked/quick-dry clothing
- [ ] Loose-fitting shirts
- [ ] Loose-fitting pants
- [ ] Hiking pants/shorts
- [ ] Short-sleeved/sleeveless shirts
- [ ] Full winter gear
- [ ] ....
- [ ] ....
- [ ] ....
- [ ] Leisurewear
- [ ] Beachwear
- [ ] Hiking shoes
- [ ] Athletic shoes
- [ ] Water shoes
- [ ] Sandals/flip-flops
- [ ] Neck gaiter
- [ ] Sun hat/cap
- [ ] Stocking cap
- [ ] Socks + extra pair
- [ ] Undergarments
- [ ] Gloves/mittens
- [ ] ....
- [ ] ....
- [ ] ....
- [ ] ....
- [ ] ....
- [ ] ....
- [ ] ....

OUTDOOR GEAR

- [ ] Hiking poles
- [ ] Tent
- [ ] Sleeping bag
- [ ] Sleeping pad
- [ ] Pillow
- [ ] Shade tent
- [ ] Emergency space blanket
- [ ] Tarp
- [ ] Daypack
- [ ] Headlamp(s)
- [ ] Lantern(s)
- [ ] Water filter & iodine tablets
- [ ] Large refillable water jug
- [ ] Portable stove
- [ ] Hot beverage thermos
- [ ] Nylon hammock
- [ ] Throw blanket
- [ ] Reusable dishes/cutlery
- [ ] Hand warmers
- [ ] ....
- [ ] ....
- [ ] ....
- [ ] ....
- [ ] ....
- [ ] ....
- [ ] ....
- [ ] ....
- [ ] ....
- [ ] ....

FOOD & DRINK

- [ ] Water
- [ ] Refillable water bottle
- [ ] Energy drinks with electrolytes
- [ ] Protein-packed snacks
- [ ] Salty, easy-to-digest snacks
- [ ] Dehydrated food
- [ ] No-cook food items
- [ ] ....
- [ ] ....
- [ ] ....
- [ ] ....
- [ ] ....
- [ ] ....
- [ ] ....
- [ ] ....
- [ ] ....
- [ ] ....
- [ ] ....
- [ ] ....
- [ ] ....
- [ ] ....
- [ ] ....
- [ ] ....

PARK-SPECIFIC

- [ ] *The National Parks Journal*!
- [ ] Permits
- [ ] Guidebooks
- [ ] Park map
- [ ] ....
- [ ] ....
- [ ] ....
- [ ] ....
- [ ] ....
- [ ] ....
- [ ] ....

MISCELLANEOUS

- [ ] Duct tape
- [ ] Multipurpose tool
- [ ] Knife
- [ ] Scissors
- [ ] Can opener
- [ ] Matches/lighter/ firestarter
- [ ] Hatchet
- [ ] Whistle
- [ ] Bandana
- [ ] Quick-dry towels
- [ ] Waterproof bags
- [ ] Ziplock bags
- [ ] Trash bags
- [ ] Paper towels
- [ ] Bear can
- [ ] Binoculars
- [ ] Deck of cards/games
- [ ] Driver's license, registration, insurance, etc.
- [ ] Spare tire/jack
- [ ] Wiper blades
- [ ] Small amount of cash
- [ ] ....
- [ ] ....
- [ ] ....
- [ ] ....
- [ ] ....
- [ ] ....
- [ ] ....
- [ ] ....
- [ ] ....
- [ ] ....
- [ ] ....
- [ ] ....
- [ ] ....
- [ ] ....

PERSONALIZED LIST

- [ ] ....
- [ ] ....
- [ ] ....
- [ ] ....
- [ ] ....
- [ ] ....
- [ ] ....
- [ ] ....
- [ ] ....
- [ ] ....
- [ ] ....

TO BUY

- [ ] ....
- [ ] ....
- [ ] ....
- [ ] ....
- [ ] ....
- [ ] ....
- [ ] ....
- [ ] ....
- [ ] ....
- [ ] ....

ADDITIONAL NOTES

RECORD YOUR TRIP!

Park name: ....

State/territory: ....

Dates visited: ....

Nearby sites visited: ....

ARROWHEAD RATING!

⬙ 5 — Epic & life-changing experience

⬙ 4 — Want to learn everything about this park!

⬙ 3 — See why this place is so special

⬙ 2 — Happy I went and had some good times

⬙ 1 — Once and done!

FAVORITE CAMPSITE OR LODGING: ....

....

PEAK EXPERIENCE: ....

....

FAVORITE ADVENTURE: ....

....

FAVORITE LOCATION: ....

....

FAVORITE PHOTO: ....

....

BEST WILDLIFE SIGHTING: ....

....

FUN THING(S) I LEARNED ABOUT THE PARK: ....

....

INTERESTING PEOPLE MET ALONG MY JOURNEY: ....

....

VALUABLE RESOURCE(S) DISCOVERED ALONG THE WAY: ....

....

FOOD I COULDN'T LIVE WITHOUT: ....

....

THE BIGGEST CHALLENGE I FACED: ....

....

I WAS MOST PREPARED WHEN: ....

....

WISH I KNEW BEFORE I WENT: ....

....

WISH I WOULD HAVE BROUGHT: ....

....

MOST USEFUL PIECE OF GEAR: ....

....

MOST VALUABLE TOOL: ....

....

MOST USEFUL PIECE OF ADVICE: ....

....

TIPS FOR OTHER TRAVELERS: ....

....

ADDITIONAL NOTES: ....

....

....

....

....

PLAN YOUR TRIP!

Park name: ....

State/territory: .... Temperature range: ....

Planned dates: .... Altitude range: ....

Time zone: .... Latitude/longitude: ....

COMMITMENT LEVEL

6 — Full throttle, all-in adventure time!
5 — Bring on a big challenge!
4 — Many trails, sites, & adventures planned!
3 — Rolling where the wind blows me!
2 — Tons to do without breaking a big sweat!
1 — Easy-going, leisurely days...

SEASON OF VISIT
- [ ] Spring
- [ ] Summer
- [ ] Autumn
- [ ] Winter

TOURING/SUPPORT
- [ ] Self-guided
- [ ] Privately guided
- [ ] Chartered trip
- [ ] Group trip
- [ ] Volunteering
- [ ] Ranger-led tours
- [ ] Instructional classes
- [ ] Special events
- [ ] ....
- [ ] ....
- [ ] ....
- [ ] ....
- [ ] ....

PARK TRANSPORT
- [ ] Car
- [ ] Bus
- [ ] RV/travel trailer
- [ ] Boat
- [ ] Float plane/bush plane
- [ ] Helicopter
- [ ] Tour bus
- [ ] All-terrain vehicle
- [ ] ....

PARK ITEMS TO PICK UP
- [ ] NPS annual pass
- [ ] NPS parks passport
- [ ] Pins, patches, & stickers
- [ ] Hiking stick medallions
- [ ] NPS maps & literature
- [ ] ....
- [ ] ....
- [ ] ....

RESOURCES/CONTACTS
- [ ] NPS visitor center(s):
....
- [ ] Wilderness permit(s):
....
- [ ] Tour company:
....
- [ ] Local guide(s):
....
- [ ] Local gear outfitter(s):
....
- [ ] Emergency services:
....
- [ ] Miscellaneous contact:
....
- [ ] Miscellaneous contact:
....

MAIN ACCOMMODATIONS
- [ ] NPS lodge
- [ ] Hotel
- [ ] RV/travel trailer
- [ ] Tent camping
- [ ] Backcountry camping
- [ ] Staying with friends
- [ ] Houseboat
- [ ] Cruise ship
- [ ] Van/car
- [ ] ....

AMENITIES

- [ ] Campgrounds
  - [ ] Standard
  - [ ] RV
  - [ ] Primitive
  - [ ] Day use only
  - [ ] Group
- [ ] Plumbed bathrooms
- [ ] Showers
- [ ] Park store
- [ ] Wi-Fi
- [ ] NPS amphitheater
- [ ] Pet-friendly
- [ ] ---------------------------------
- [ ] ---------------------------------

IN-TOW

- [ ] Spouse/partner
- [ ] Children
- [ ] Pets
- [ ] Friends
- [ ] Extended family
- [ ] Boatloads of gear!
- [ ] ---------------------------------
- [ ] ---------------------------------

ADVANCED PLANNING

- [ ] Physical training?

- [ ] Seasonal aspects?

- [ ] Obtained permits?

- [ ] Purchased gear?

FINAL SAFETY CHECKS

- [ ] Left your trip plan with an emergency contact back home?
- [ ] Reviewed basic emergency aid procedures?
- [ ] Additional forms/permits needed?
- [ ] Checked on closures/mandates that might affect your travel?
- [ ] ---------------------------------
- [ ] ---------------------------------
- [ ] ---------------------------------

MAIN GOALS

- [ ] Solitude
- [ ] Active adventure
- [ ] Creative pursuits
- [ ] Learning
- [ ] Endurance training
- [ ] Gathering loved ones
- [ ] Seeing new things!
- [ ] ---------------------------------
- [ ] ---------------------------------
- [ ] ---------------------------------

IMMERSIVE EXPERIENCES

- [ ] Cultural/historical
- [ ] Volunteering
- [ ] Park programs
- [ ] Junior Ranger program
- [ ] NPS-guided night walks
- [ ] School/youth trips
- [ ] Teacher/educator programs
- [ ] Professional development
- [ ] ---------------------------------
- [ ] ---------------------------------
- [ ] ---------------------------------

ADVENTURE GOALS

- [ ] Hiking big trails
- [ ] Easy day hikes
- [ ] Cycling/mountain biking/fat biking
- [ ] Kayaking/canoeing/SUP
- [ ] Trail running
- [ ] Rafting
- [ ] Swimming
- [ ] Backpacking
- [ ] Wildlife viewing
- [ ] Scenic drives
- [ ] Fishing/angling
- [ ] Mountaineering
- [ ] Climbing/bouldering
- [ ] Photography
- [ ] Birdwatching
- [ ] Stargazing
- [ ] Cultural immersion
- [ ] Endurance training
- [ ] Picnicking
- [ ] ---------------------------------

PHOTOGRAPHY PLANS

- [ ] Wildlife
- [ ] Birds
- [ ] Landscapes
- [ ] Night skies
- [ ] People
- [ ] Cultural artifacts
- [ ] Macro/abstract
- [ ] Family pictures
- [ ] Selfies
- [ ] ---------------------------------

ADDITIONAL NOTES

PACK FOR YOUR TRIP!

Park name: ....

HEALTH & PERSONAL ITEMS

- ☐ Premade first aid kit
- ☐ Wildlife/insect protection
- ☐ Medications
- ☐ ....
- ☐ ....
- ☐ Supplements
- ☐ ....
- ☐ ....
- ☐ Eyeglasses/contacts
- ☐ Sun/wind/snow protection (eyes/skin/face)
- ☐ Facial tissues
- ☐ Bug spray
- ☐ Antibacterial wipes
- ☐ ....
- ☐ ....

ELECTRONICS

- ☐ Camera
  - ☐ Tripod
  - ☐ Lenses/lens cloths
  - ☐ Memory cards
  - ☐ Batteries & charger
- ☐ Weather protection
- ☐ External charging device
- ☐ Phone & charging cord
- ☐ Mobile Wi-Fi device
- ☐ Electronic tablet
- ☐ Satellite phone
- ☐ Personal locater beacon
- ☐ ....

CLOTHING/SHOES

- ☐ Insulated jacket
- ☐ Rain jacket/pants
- ☐ Thermal layers
- ☐ Wicked/quick-dry clothing
- ☐ Loose-fitting shirts
- ☐ Loose-fitting pants
- ☐ Hiking pants/shorts
- ☐ Short-sleeved/sleeveless shirts
- ☐ Full winter gear
- ☐ ....
- ☐ ....
- ☐ ....
- ☐ Leisurewear
- ☐ Beachwear
- ☐ Hiking shoes
- ☐ Athletic shoes
- ☐ Water shoes
- ☐ Sandals/flip-flops
- ☐ Neck gaiter
- ☐ Sun hat/cap
- ☐ Stocking cap
- ☐ Socks + extra pair
- ☐ Undergarments
- ☐ Gloves/mittens
- ☐ ....
- ☐ ....
- ☐ ....
- ☐ ....
- ☐ ....
- ☐ ....

OUTDOOR GEAR

- ☐ Hiking poles
- ☐ Tent
- ☐ Sleeping bag
- ☐ Sleeping pad
- ☐ Pillow
- ☐ Shade tent
- ☐ Emergency space blanket
- ☐ Tarp
- ☐ Daypack
- ☐ Headlamp(s)
- ☐ Lantern(s)
- ☐ Water filter & iodine tablets
- ☐ Large refillable water jug
- ☐ Portable stove
- ☐ Hot beverage thermos
- ☐ Nylon hammock
- ☐ Throw blanket
- ☐ Reusable dishes/cutlery
- ☐ Hand warmers
- ☐ ....
- ☐ ....
- ☐ ....
- ☐ ....
- ☐ ....
- ☐ ....
- ☐ ....
- ☐ ....
- ☐ ....
- ☐ ....

FOOD & DRINK

- [ ] Water
- [ ] Refillable water bottle
- [ ] Energy drinks with electrolytes
- [ ] Protein-packed snacks
- [ ] Salty, easy-to-digest snacks
- [ ] Dehydrated food
- [ ] No-cook food items
- [ ] ....
- [ ] ....
- [ ] ....
- [ ] ....
- [ ] ....
- [ ] ....
- [ ] ....
- [ ] ....
- [ ] ....
- [ ] ....
- [ ] ....
- [ ] ....
- [ ] ....
- [ ] ....
- [ ] ....

PARK-SPECIFIC

- [ ] *The National Parks Journal*!
- [ ] Permits
- [ ] Guidebooks
- [ ] Park map
- [ ] ....
- [ ] ....
- [ ] ....
- [ ] ....
- [ ] ....
- [ ] ....
- [ ] ....

MISCELLANEOUS

- [ ] Duct tape
- [ ] Multipurpose tool
- [ ] Knife
- [ ] Scissors
- [ ] Can opener
- [ ] Matches/lighter/ firestarter
- [ ] Hatchet
- [ ] Whistle
- [ ] Bandana
- [ ] Quick-dry towels
- [ ] Waterproof bags
- [ ] Ziplock bags
- [ ] Trash bags
- [ ] Paper towels
- [ ] Bear can
- [ ] Binoculars
- [ ] Deck of cards/games
- [ ] Driver's license, registration, insurance, etc.
- [ ] Spare tire/jack
- [ ] Wiper blades
- [ ] Small amount of cash
- [ ] ....
- [ ] ....
- [ ] ....
- [ ] ....
- [ ] ....
- [ ] ....
- [ ] ....
- [ ] ....
- [ ] ....
- [ ] ....
- [ ] ....
- [ ] ....
- [ ] ....
- [ ] ....

PERSONALIZED LIST

- [ ] ....
- [ ] ....
- [ ] ....
- [ ] ....
- [ ] ....
- [ ] ....
- [ ] ....
- [ ] ....
- [ ] ....
- [ ] ....

TO BUY

- [ ] ....
- [ ] ....
- [ ] ....
- [ ] ....
- [ ] ....
- [ ] ....
- [ ] ....
- [ ] ....
- [ ] ....
- [ ] ....

ADDITIONAL NOTES

RECORD YOUR TRIP!

Park name: ....

State/territory: ....

Dates visited: ....

Nearby sites visited: ....

ARROWHEAD RATING!

- 5 — Epic & life-changing experience
- 4 — Want to learn everything about this park!
- 3 — See why this place is so special
- 2 — Happy I went and had some good times
- 1 — Once and done!

FAVORITE CAMPSITE OR LODGING: ....

....

PEAK EXPERIENCE: ....

....

FAVORITE ADVENTURE: ....

....

FAVORITE LOCATION: ....

....

FAVORITE PHOTO: ....

....

BEST WILDLIFE SIGHTING: ....

....

FUN THING(S) I LEARNED ABOUT THE PARK: ....

....

INTERESTING PEOPLE MET ALONG MY JOURNEY: --

VALUABLE RESOURCE(S) DISCOVERED ALONG THE WAY: --------------------------------------
----

FOOD I COULDN'T LIVE WITHOUT: --

THE BIGGEST CHALLENGE I FACED: ---

I WAS MOST PREPARED WHEN: --

WISH I KNEW BEFORE I WENT: --

WISH I WOULD HAVE BROUGHT: ---

MOST USEFUL PIECE OF GEAR: --

MOST VALUABLE TOOL: ---

MOST USEFUL PIECE OF ADVICE: --

TIPS FOR OTHER TRAVELERS: ---

ADDITIONAL NOTES: ---

PLAN YOUR TRIP!

Park name: ....

State/territory: ....   Temperature range: ....

Planned dates: ....   Altitude range: ....

Time zone: ....   Latitude/longitude: ....

COMMITMENT LEVEL

- 6 — Full throttle, all-in adventure time!
- 5 — Bring on a big challenge!
- 4 — Many trails, sites, & adventures planned!
- 3 — Rolling where the wind blows me!
- 2 — Tons to do without breaking a big sweat!
- 1 — Easy-going, leisurely days...

SEASON OF VISIT
- ☐ Spring
- ☐ Summer
- ☐ Autumn
- ☐ Winter

TOURING/SUPPORT
- ☐ Self-guided
- ☐ Privately guided
- ☐ Chartered trip
- ☐ Group trip
- ☐ Volunteering
- ☐ Ranger-led tours
- ☐ Instructional classes
- ☐ Special events
- ....
- ....
- ....
- ....
- ....

PARK TRANSPORT
- ☐ Car
- ☐ Bus
- ☐ RV/travel trailer
- ☐ Boat
- ☐ Float plane/bush plane
- ☐ Helicopter
- ☐ Tour bus
- ☐ All-terrain vehicle
- ☐ ....

PARK ITEMS TO PICK UP
- ☐ NPS annual pass
- ☐ NPS parks passport
- ☐ Pins, patches, & stickers
- ☐ Hiking stick medallions
- ☐ NPS maps & literature
- ☐ ....
- ☐ ....
- ☐ ....

RESOURCES/CONTACTS
- ☐ NPS visitor center(s):
- ☐ Wilderness permit(s):
- ☐ Tour company:
- ☐ Local guide(s):
- ☐ Local gear outfitter(s):
- ☐ Emergency services:
- ☐ Miscellaneous contact:
- ☐ Miscellaneous contact:

MAIN ACCOMMODATIONS
- ☐ NPS lodge
- ☐ Hotel
- ☐ RV/travel trailer
- ☐ Tent camping
- ☐ Backcountry camping
- ☐ Staying with friends
- ☐ Houseboat
- ☐ Cruise ship
- ☐ Van/car
- ☐ ....
- ☐ ....

AMENITIES

- [ ] Campgrounds
  - [ ] Standard
  - [ ] RV
  - [ ] Primitive
  - [ ] Day use only
  - [ ] Group
- [ ] Plumbed bathrooms
- [ ] Showers
- [ ] Park store
- [ ] Wi-Fi
- [ ] NPS amphitheater
- [ ] Pet-friendly
- [ ] --
- [ ] --

IN-TOW

- [ ] Spouse/partner
- [ ] Children
- [ ] Pets
- [ ] Friends
- [ ] Extended family
- [ ] Boatloads of gear!
- [ ] --
- [ ] --

ADVANCED PLANNING

- [ ] Physical training?

- [ ] Seasonal aspects?

- [ ] Obtained permits?

- [ ] Purchased gear?

FINAL SAFETY CHECKS

- [ ] Left your trip plan with an emergency contact back home?
- [ ] Reviewed basic emergency aid procedures?
- [ ] Additional forms/permits needed?
- [ ] Checked on closures/mandates that might affect your travel?
- [ ] --
- [ ] --
- [ ] --

MAIN GOALS

- [ ] Solitude
- [ ] Active adventure
- [ ] Creative pursuits
- [ ] Learning
- [ ] Endurance training
- [ ] Gathering loved ones
- [ ] Seeing new things!
- [ ] --
- [ ] --
- [ ] --

IMMERSIVE EXPERIENCES

- [ ] Cultural/historical
- [ ] Volunteering
- [ ] Park programs
- [ ] Junior Ranger program
- [ ] NPS-guided night walks
- [ ] School/youth trips
- [ ] Teacher/educator programs
- [ ] Professional development
- [ ] --
- [ ] --
- [ ] --

ADVENTURE GOALS

- [ ] Hiking big trails
- [ ] Easy day hikes
- [ ] Cycling/mountain biking/fat biking
- [ ] Kayaking/canoeing/SUP
- [ ] Trail running
- [ ] Rafting
- [ ] Swimming
- [ ] Backpacking
- [ ] Wildlife viewing
- [ ] Scenic drives
- [ ] Fishing/angling
- [ ] Mountaineering
- [ ] Climbing/bouldering
- [ ] Photography
- [ ] Birdwatching
- [ ] Stargazing
- [ ] Cultural immersion
- [ ] Endurance training
- [ ] Picnicking
- [ ] --

PHOTOGRAPHY PLANS

- [ ] Wildlife
- [ ] Birds
- [ ] Landscapes
- [ ] Night skies
- [ ] People
- [ ] Cultural artifacts
- [ ] Macro/abstract
- [ ] Family pictures
- [ ] Selfies
- [ ] --

ADDITIONAL NOTES

PACK FOR YOUR TRIP!

Park name: ....

HEALTH & PERSONAL ITEMS
- [ ] Premade first aid kit
- [ ] Wildlife/insect protection
- [ ] Medications
- [ ] ....
- [ ] ....
- [ ] Supplements
- [ ] ....
- [ ] ....
- [ ] Eyeglasses/contacts
- [ ] Sun/wind/snow protection (eyes/skin/face)
- [ ] Facial tissues
- [ ] Bug spray
- [ ] Antibacterial wipes
- [ ] ....
- [ ] ....

ELECTRONICS
- [ ] Camera
  - [ ] Tripod
  - [ ] Lenses/lens cloths
  - [ ] Memory cards
  - [ ] Batteries & charger
- [ ] Weather protection
- [ ] External charging device
- [ ] Phone & charging cord
- [ ] Mobile Wi-Fi device
- [ ] Electronic tablet
- [ ] Satellite phone
- [ ] Personal locater beacon
- [ ] ....

CLOTHING/SHOES
- [ ] Insulated jacket
- [ ] Rain jacket/pants
- [ ] Thermal layers
- [ ] Wicked/quick-dry clothing
- [ ] Loose-fitting shirts
- [ ] Loose-fitting pants
- [ ] Hiking pants/shorts
- [ ] Short-sleeved/sleeveless shirts
- [ ] Full winter gear
- [ ] ....
- [ ] ....
- [ ] ....
- [ ] Leisurewear
- [ ] Beachwear
- [ ] Hiking shoes
- [ ] Athletic shoes
- [ ] Water shoes
- [ ] Sandals/flip-flops
- [ ] Neck gaiter
- [ ] Sun hat/cap
- [ ] Stocking cap
- [ ] Socks + extra pair
- [ ] Undergarments
- [ ] Gloves/mittens
- [ ] ....
- [ ] ....
- [ ] ....
- [ ] ....
- [ ] ....
- [ ] ....
- [ ] ....

OUTDOOR GEAR
- [ ] Hiking poles
- [ ] Tent
- [ ] Sleeping bag
- [ ] Sleeping pad
- [ ] Pillow
- [ ] Shade tent
- [ ] Emergency space blanket
- [ ] Tarp
- [ ] Daypack
- [ ] Headlamp(s)
- [ ] Lantern(s)
- [ ] Water filter & iodine tablets
- [ ] Large refillable water jug
- [ ] Portable stove
- [ ] Hot beverage thermos
- [ ] Nylon hammock
- [ ] Throw blanket
- [ ] Reusable dishes/cutlery
- [ ] Hand warmers
- [ ] ....
- [ ] ....
- [ ] ....
- [ ] ....
- [ ] ....
- [ ] ....
- [ ] ....
- [ ] ....
- [ ] ....

FOOD & DRINK

- [ ] Water
- [ ] Refillable water bottle
- [ ] Energy drinks with electrolytes
- [ ] Protein-packed snacks
- [ ] Salty, easy-to-digest snacks
- [ ] Dehydrated food
- [ ] No-cook food items
- [ ] _____
- [ ] _____
- [ ] _____
- [ ] _____
- [ ] _____
- [ ] _____
- [ ] _____
- [ ] _____
- [ ] _____
- [ ] _____
- [ ] _____
- [ ] _____
- [ ] _____
- [ ] _____
- [ ] _____
- [ ] _____

PARK-SPECIFIC

- [ ] *The National Parks Journal*!
- [ ] Permits
- [ ] Guidebooks
- [ ] Park map
- [ ] _____
- [ ] _____
- [ ] _____
- [ ] _____
- [ ] _____
- [ ] _____

MISCELLANEOUS

- [ ] Duct tape
- [ ] Multipurpose tool
- [ ] Knife
- [ ] Scissors
- [ ] Can opener
- [ ] Matches/lighter/firestarter
- [ ] Hatchet
- [ ] Whistle
- [ ] Bandana
- [ ] Quick-dry towels
- [ ] Waterproof bags
- [ ] Ziplock bags
- [ ] Trash bags
- [ ] Paper towels
- [ ] Bear can
- [ ] Binoculars
- [ ] Deck of cards/games
- [ ] Driver's license, registration, insurance, etc.
- [ ] Spare tire/jack
- [ ] Wiper blades
- [ ] Small amount of cash
- [ ] _____
- [ ] _____
- [ ] _____
- [ ] _____
- [ ] _____
- [ ] _____
- [ ] _____
- [ ] _____
- [ ] _____
- [ ] _____
- [ ] _____
- [ ] _____
- [ ] _____
- [ ] _____

PERSONALIZED LIST

- [ ] _____
- [ ] _____
- [ ] _____
- [ ] _____
- [ ] _____
- [ ] _____
- [ ] _____
- [ ] _____
- [ ] _____
- [ ] _____

TO BUY

- [ ] _____
- [ ] _____
- [ ] _____
- [ ] _____
- [ ] _____
- [ ] _____
- [ ] _____
- [ ] _____
- [ ] _____
- [ ] _____

ADDITIONAL NOTES

RECORD YOUR TRIP!

Park name: ....

State/territory: ....

Dates visited: ....

Nearby sites visited: ....

ARROWHEAD RATING!

- 5 — Epic & life-changing experience
- 4 — Want to learn everything about this park!
- 3 — See why this place is so special
- 2 — Happy I went and had some good times
- 1 — Once and done!

FAVORITE CAMPSITE OR LODGING: ....

....

PEAK EXPERIENCE: ....

....

FAVORITE ADVENTURE: ....

....

FAVORITE LOCATION: ....

....

FAVORITE PHOTO: ....

....

BEST WILDLIFE SIGHTING: ....

....

FUN THING(S) I LEARNED ABOUT THE PARK: ....

....

INTERESTING PEOPLE MET ALONG MY JOURNEY: --

VALUABLE RESOURCE(S) DISCOVERED ALONG THE WAY: ---

FOOD I COULDN'T LIVE WITHOUT: ---

THE BIGGEST CHALLENGE I FACED: --

I WAS MOST PREPARED WHEN: --

WISH I KNEW BEFORE I WENT: ---

WISH I WOULD HAVE BROUGHT: ---

MOST USEFUL PIECE OF GEAR: ---

MOST VALUABLE TOOL: --

MOST USEFUL PIECE OF ADVICE: ---

TIPS FOR OTHER TRAVELERS: --

ADDITIONAL NOTES: --

PLAN YOUR TRIP!

Park name: ....

State/territory: ....   Temperature range: ....

Planned dates: ....   Altitude range: ....

Time zone: ....   Latitude/longitude: ....

COMMITMENT LEVEL

- 6 — Full throttle, all-in adventure time!
- 5 — Bring on a big challenge!
- 4 — Many trails, sites, & adventures planned!
- 3 — Rolling where the wind blows me!
- 2 — Tons to do without breaking a big sweat!
- 1 — Easy-going, leisurely days...

SEASON OF VISIT

- ☐ Spring
- ☐ Summer
- ☐ Autumn
- ☐ Winter

TOURING/SUPPORT

- ☐ Self-guided
- ☐ Privately guided
- ☐ Chartered trip
- ☐ Group trip
- ☐ Volunteering
- ☐ Ranger-led tours
- ☐ Instructional classes
- ☐ Special events
- ☐ ....
- ☐ ....
- ☐ ....
- ☐ ....
- ☐ ....

PARK TRANSPORT

- ☐ Car
- ☐ Bus
- ☐ RV/travel trailer
- ☐ Boat
- ☐ Float plane/bush plane
- ☐ Helicopter
- ☐ Tour bus
- ☐ All-terrain vehicle
- ☐ ....

PARK ITEMS TO PICK UP

- ☐ NPS annual pass
- ☐ NPS parks passport
- ☐ Pins, patches, & stickers
- ☐ Hiking stick medallions
- ☐ NPS maps & literature
- ☐ ....
- ☐ ....
- ☐ ....

RESOURCES/CONTACTS

- ☐ NPS visitor center(s): ....
- ☐ Wilderness permit(s): ....
- ☐ Tour company: ....
- ☐ Local guide(s): ....
- ☐ Local gear outfitter(s): ....
- ☐ Emergency services: ....
- ☐ Miscellaneous contact: ....
- ☐ Miscellaneous contact: ....

MAIN ACCOMMODATIONS

- ☐ NPS lodge
- ☐ Hotel
- ☐ RV/travel trailer
- ☐ Tent camping
- ☐ Backcountry camping
- ☐ Staying with friends
- ☐ Houseboat
- ☐ Cruise ship
- ☐ Van/car
- ☐ ....
- ☐ ....

AMENITIES

- [ ] Campgrounds
  - [ ] Standard
  - [ ] RV
  - [ ] Primitive
  - [ ] Day use only
  - [ ] Group
- [ ] Plumbed bathrooms
- [ ] Showers
- [ ] Park store
- [ ] Wi-Fi
- [ ] NPS amphitheater
- [ ] Pet-friendly
- [ ] --------------------------------
- [ ] --------------------------------

IN-TOW

- [ ] Spouse/partner
- [ ] Children
- [ ] Pets
- [ ] Friends
- [ ] Extended family
- [ ] Boatloads of gear!
- [ ] --------------------------------
- [ ] --------------------------------

ADVANCED PLANNING

- [ ] Physical training?

- [ ] Seasonal aspects?

- [ ] Obtained permits?

- [ ] Purchased gear?

FINAL SAFETY CHECKS

- [ ] Left your trip plan with an emergency contact back home?
- [ ] Reviewed basic emergency aid procedures?
- [ ] Additional forms/permits needed?
- [ ] Checked on closures/mandates that might affect your travel?
- [ ] --------------------------------
- [ ] --------------------------------
- [ ] --------------------------------

MAIN GOALS

- [ ] Solitude
- [ ] Active adventure
- [ ] Creative pursuits
- [ ] Learning
- [ ] Endurance training
- [ ] Gathering loved ones
- [ ] Seeing new things!
- [ ] --------------------------------
- [ ] --------------------------------
- [ ] --------------------------------

IMMERSIVE EXPERIENCES

- [ ] Cultural/historical
- [ ] Volunteering
- [ ] Park programs
- [ ] Junior Ranger program
- [ ] NPS-guided night walks
- [ ] School/youth trips
- [ ] Teacher/educator programs
- [ ] Professional development
- [ ] --------------------------------
- [ ] --------------------------------
- [ ] --------------------------------

ADVENTURE GOALS

- [ ] Hiking big trails
- [ ] Easy day hikes
- [ ] Cycling/mountain biking/fat biking
- [ ] Kayaking/canoeing/SUP
- [ ] Trail running
- [ ] Rafting
- [ ] Swimming
- [ ] Backpacking
- [ ] Wildlife viewing
- [ ] Scenic drives
- [ ] Fishing/angling
- [ ] Mountaineering
- [ ] Climbing/bouldering
- [ ] Photography
- [ ] Birdwatching
- [ ] Stargazing
- [ ] Cultural immersion
- [ ] Endurance training
- [ ] Picnicking
- [ ] --------------------------------

PHOTOGRAPHY PLANS

- [ ] Wildlife
- [ ] Birds
- [ ] Landscapes
- [ ] Night skies
- [ ] People
- [ ] Cultural artifacts
- [ ] Macro/abstract
- [ ] Family pictures
- [ ] Selfies
- [ ] --------------------------------

ADDITIONAL NOTES

PACK FOR YOUR TRIP!

Park name: ....

HEALTH & PERSONAL ITEMS

- ☐ Premade first aid kit
- ☐ Wildlife/insect protection
- ☐ Medications
- ☐ ....
- ☐ ....
- ☐ Supplements
- ☐ ....
- ☐ ....
- ☐ Eyeglasses/contacts
- ☐ Sun/wind/snow protection (eyes/skin/face)
- ☐ Facial tissues
- ☐ Bug spray
- ☐ Antibacterial wipes
- ☐ ....
- ☐ ....

ELECTRONICS

- ☐ Camera
  - ☐ Tripod
  - ☐ Lenses/lens cloths
  - ☐ Memory cards
  - ☐ Batteries & charger
- ☐ Weather protection
- ☐ External charging device
- ☐ Phone & charging cord
- ☐ Mobile Wi-Fi device
- ☐ Electronic tablet
- ☐ Satellite phone
- ☐ Personal locater beacon
- ☐ ....

CLOTHING/SHOES

- ☐ Insulated jacket
- ☐ Rain jacket/pants
- ☐ Thermal layers
- ☐ Wicked/quick-dry clothing
- ☐ Loose-fitting shirts
- ☐ Loose-fitting pants
- ☐ Hiking pants/shorts
- ☐ Short-sleeved/sleeveless shirts
- ☐ Full winter gear
- ☐ ....
- ☐ ....
- ☐ ....
- ☐ Leisurewear
- ☐ Beachwear
- ☐ Hiking shoes
- ☐ Athletic shoes
- ☐ Water shoes
- ☐ Sandals/flip-flops
- ☐ Neck gaiter
- ☐ Sun hat/cap
- ☐ Stocking cap
- ☐ Socks + extra pair
- ☐ Undergarments
- ☐ Gloves/mittens
- ☐ ....
- ☐ ....
- ☐ ....
- ☐ ....
- ☐ ....
- ☐ ....
- ☐ ....

OUTDOOR GEAR

- ☐ Hiking poles
- ☐ Tent
- ☐ Sleeping bag
- ☐ Sleeping pad
- ☐ Pillow
- ☐ Shade tent
- ☐ Emergency space blanket
- ☐ Tarp
- ☐ Daypack
- ☐ Headlamp(s)
- ☐ Lantern(s)
- ☐ Water filter & iodine tablets
- ☐ Large refillable water jug
- ☐ Portable stove
- ☐ Hot beverage thermos
- ☐ Nylon hammock
- ☐ Throw blanket
- ☐ Reusable dishes/cutlery
- ☐ Hand warmers
- ☐ ....
- ☐ ....
- ☐ ....
- ☐ ....
- ☐ ....
- ☐ ....
- ☐ ....
- ☐ ....
- ☐ ....
- ☐ ....
- ☐ ....

FOOD & DRINK

- [ ] Water
- [ ] Refillable water bottle
- [ ] Energy drinks with electrolytes
- [ ] Protein-packed snacks
- [ ] Salty, easy-to-digest snacks
- [ ] Dehydrated food
- [ ] No-cook food items
- [ ] ------------------------------
- [ ] ------------------------------
- [ ] ------------------------------
- [ ] ------------------------------
- [ ] ------------------------------
- [ ] ------------------------------
- [ ] ------------------------------
- [ ] ------------------------------
- [ ] ------------------------------
- [ ] ------------------------------
- [ ] ------------------------------
- [ ] ------------------------------
- [ ] ------------------------------
- [ ] ------------------------------
- [ ] ------------------------------

PARK-SPECIFIC

- [ ] *The National Parks Journal*!
- [ ] Permits
- [ ] Guidebooks
- [ ] Park map
- [ ] ------------------------------
- [ ] ------------------------------
- [ ] ------------------------------
- [ ] ------------------------------
- [ ] ------------------------------
- [ ] ------------------------------
- [ ] ------------------------------

MISCELLANEOUS

- [ ] Duct tape
- [ ] Multipurpose tool
- [ ] Knife
- [ ] Scissors
- [ ] Can opener
- [ ] Matches/lighter/firestarter
- [ ] Hatchet
- [ ] Whistle
- [ ] Bandana
- [ ] Quick-dry towels
- [ ] Waterproof bags
- [ ] Ziplock bags
- [ ] Trash bags
- [ ] Paper towels
- [ ] Bear can
- [ ] Binoculars
- [ ] Deck of cards/games
- [ ] Driver's license, registration, insurance, etc.
- [ ] Spare tire/jack
- [ ] Wiper blades
- [ ] Small amount of cash
- [ ] ------------------------------
- [ ] ------------------------------
- [ ] ------------------------------
- [ ] ------------------------------
- [ ] ------------------------------
- [ ] ------------------------------
- [ ] ------------------------------
- [ ] ------------------------------
- [ ] ------------------------------
- [ ] ------------------------------
- [ ] ------------------------------
- [ ] ------------------------------
- [ ] ------------------------------
- [ ] ------------------------------
- [ ] ------------------------------

PERSONALIZED LIST

- [ ] ------------------------------
- [ ] ------------------------------
- [ ] ------------------------------
- [ ] ------------------------------
- [ ] ------------------------------
- [ ] ------------------------------
- [ ] ------------------------------
- [ ] ------------------------------
- [ ] ------------------------------
- [ ] ------------------------------
- [ ] ------------------------------

TO BUY

- [ ] ------------------------------
- [ ] ------------------------------
- [ ] ------------------------------
- [ ] ------------------------------
- [ ] ------------------------------
- [ ] ------------------------------
- [ ] ------------------------------
- [ ] ------------------------------
- [ ] ------------------------------
- [ ] ------------------------------

ADDITIONAL NOTES

RECORD YOUR TRIP!

Park name: ....

State/territory: ....

Dates visited: ....

Nearby sites visited: ....

ARROWHEAD RATING!

5 — Epic & life-changing experience

4 — Want to learn everything about this park!

3 — See why this place is so special

2 — Happy I went and had some good times

1 — Once and done!

FAVORITE CAMPSITE OR LODGING: ....

....

PEAK EXPERIENCE: ....

....

FAVORITE ADVENTURE: ....

....

FAVORITE LOCATION: ....

....

FAVORITE PHOTO: ....

....

BEST WILDLIFE SIGHTING: ....

....

FUN THING(S) I LEARNED ABOUT THE PARK: ....

....

INTERESTING PEOPLE MET ALONG MY JOURNEY: --

VALUABLE RESOURCE(S) DISCOVERED ALONG THE WAY: ---------------------------------------

----

FOOD I COULDN'T LIVE WITHOUT: --

THE BIGGEST CHALLENGE I FACED: ---

I WAS MOST PREPARED WHEN: ---

WISH I KNEW BEFORE I WENT: --

WISH I WOULD HAVE BROUGHT: ---

MOST USEFUL PIECE OF GEAR: --

MOST VALUABLE TOOL: --

MOST USEFUL PIECE OF ADVICE: ---

TIPS FOR OTHER TRAVELERS: ---

ADDITIONAL NOTES: ---

PLAN YOUR TRIP!

Park name: ....

State/territory: .... Temperature range: ....

Planned dates: .... Altitude range: ....

Time zone: .... Latitude/longitude: ....

COMMITMENT LEVEL

6 — Full throttle, all-in adventure time!

5 — Bring on a big challenge!

4 — Many trails, sites, & adventures planned!

3 — Rolling where the wind blows me!

2 — Tons to do without breaking a big sweat!

1 — Easy-going, leisurely days...

SEASON OF VISIT

☐ Spring
☐ Summer
☐ Autumn
☐ Winter

TOURING/SUPPORT

☐ Self-guided
☐ Privately guided
☐ Chartered trip
☐ Group trip
☐ Volunteering
☐ Ranger-led tours
☐ Instructional classes
☐ Special events
....
....
....
....
....

PARK TRANSPORT

☐ Car
☐ Bus
☐ RV/travel trailer
☐ Boat
☐ Float plane/bush plane
☐ Helicopter
☐ Tour bus
☐ All-terrain vehicle
☐ ....

PARK ITEMS TO PICK UP

☐ NPS annual pass
☐ NPS parks passport
☐ Pins, patches, & stickers
☐ Hiking stick medallions
☐ NPS maps & literature
☐ ....
☐ ....
☐ ....

RESOURCES/CONTACTS

☐ NPS visitor center(s):
....
☐ Wilderness permit(s):
....
☐ Tour company:
....
☐ Local guide(s):
....
☐ Local gear outfitter(s):
....
☐ Emergency services:
....
☐ Miscellaneous contact:
....
☐ Miscellaneous contact:
....

MAIN ACCOMMODATIONS

☐ NPS lodge
☐ Hotel
☐ RV/travel trailer
☐ Tent camping
☐ Backcountry camping
☐ Staying with friends
☐ Houseboat
☐ Cruise ship
☐ Van/car
☐ ....
☐ ....

AMENITIES

- ☐ Campgrounds
  - ☐ Standard
  - ☐ RV
  - ☐ Primitive
  - ☐ Day use only
  - ☐ Group
- ☐ Plumbed bathrooms
- ☐ Showers
- ☐ Park store
- ☐ Wi-Fi
- ☐ NPS amphitheater
- ☐ Pet-friendly
- ☐ ....
- ☐ ....

IN-TOW

- ☐ Spouse/partner
- ☐ Children
- ☐ Pets
- ☐ Friends
- ☐ Extended family
- ☐ Boatloads of gear!
- ☐ ....
- ☐ ....

ADVANCED PLANNING

- ☐ Physical training?

  ....

  ....
- ☐ Seasonal aspects?

  ....

  ....
- ☐ Obtained permits?

  ....

  ....
- ☐ Purchased gear?

  ....

  ....

  ....

FINAL SAFETY CHECKS

- ☐ Left your trip plan with an emergency contact back home?
- ☐ Reviewed basic emergency aid procedures?
- ☐ Additional forms/permits needed?
- ☐ Checked on closures/mandates that might affect your travel?
- ☐ ....
- ☐ ....
- ☐ ....

MAIN GOALS

- ☐ Solitude
- ☐ Active adventure
- ☐ Creative pursuits
- ☐ Learning
- ☐ Endurance training
- ☐ Gathering loved ones
- ☐ Seeing new things!
- ☐ ....
- ☐ ....
- ☐ ....

IMMERSIVE EXPERIENCES

- ☐ Cultural/historical
- ☐ Volunteering
- ☐ Park programs
- ☐ Junior Ranger program
- ☐ NPS-guided night walks
- ☐ School/youth trips
- ☐ Teacher/educator programs
- ☐ Professional development
- ☐ ....
- ☐ ....
- ☐ ....

ADVENTURE GOALS

- ☐ Hiking big trails
- ☐ Easy day hikes
- ☐ Cycling/mountain biking/fat biking
- ☐ Kayaking/canoeing/SUP
- ☐ Trail running
- ☐ Rafting
- ☐ Swimming
- ☐ Backpacking
- ☐ Wildlife viewing
- ☐ Scenic drives
- ☐ Fishing/angling
- ☐ Mountaineering
- ☐ Climbing/bouldering
- ☐ Photography
- ☐ Birdwatching
- ☐ Stargazing
- ☐ Cultural immersion
- ☐ Endurance training
- ☐ Picnicking
- ☐ ....

PHOTOGRAPHY PLANS

- ☐ Wildlife
- ☐ Birds
- ☐ Landscapes
- ☐ Night skies
- ☐ People
- ☐ Cultural artifacts
- ☐ Macro/abstract
- ☐ Family pictures
- ☐ Selfies
- ☐ ....

ADDITIONAL NOTES

....
....
....
....

PACK FOR YOUR TRIP!

Park name: ....

- ☐ Premade first aid kit
- ☐ Wildlife/insect protection
- ☐ Medications
- ☐ ....
- ☐ ....
- ☐ Supplements
- ☐ ....
- ☐ Eyeglasses/contacts
- ☐ Sun/wind/snow protection (eyes/skin/face)
- ☐ Facial tissues
- ☐ Bug spray
- ☐ Antibacterial wipes
- ☐ ....
- ☐ ....

ELECTRONICS

- ☐ Camera
  - ☐ Tripod
  - ☐ Lenses/lens cloths
  - ☐ Memory cards
  - ☐ Batteries & charger
- ☐ Weather protection
- ☐ External charging device
- ☐ Phone & charging cord
- ☐ Mobile Wi-Fi device
- ☐ Electronic tablet
- ☐ Satellite phone
- ☐ Personal locater beacon
- ☐ ....

CLOTHING/SHOES

- ☐ Insulated jacket
- ☐ Rain jacket/pants
- ☐ Thermal layers
- ☐ Wicked/quick-dry clothing
- ☐ Loose-fitting shirts
- ☐ Loose-fitting pants
- ☐ Hiking pants/shorts
- ☐ Short-sleeved/sleeveless shirts
- ☐ Full winter gear
- ☐ ....
- ☐ ....
- ☐ ....
- ☐ Leisurewear
- ☐ Beachwear
- ☐ Hiking shoes
- ☐ Athletic shoes
- ☐ Water shoes
- ☐ Sandals/flip-flops
- ☐ Neck gaiter
- ☐ Sun hat/cap
- ☐ Stocking cap
- ☐ Socks + extra pair
- ☐ Undergarments
- ☐ Gloves/mittens
- ☐ ....
- ☐ ....
- ☐ ....
- ☐ ....
- ☐ ....
- ☐ ....
- ☐ ....

OUTDOOR GEAR

- ☐ Hiking poles
- ☐ Tent
- ☐ Sleeping bag
- ☐ Sleeping pad
- ☐ Pillow
- ☐ Shade tent
- ☐ Emergency space blanket
- ☐ Tarp
- ☐ Daypack
- ☐ Headlamp(s)
- ☐ Lantern(s)
- ☐ Water filter & iodine tablets
- ☐ Large refillable water jug
- ☐ Portable stove
- ☐ Hot beverage thermos
- ☐ Nylon hammock
- ☐ Throw blanket
- ☐ Reusable dishes/cutlery
- ☐ Hand warmers
- ☐ ....
- ☐ ....
- ☐ ....
- ☐ ....
- ☐ ....
- ☐ ....
- ☐ ....
- ☐ ....
- ☐ ....

FOOD & DRINK

- [ ] Water
- [ ] Refillable water bottle
- [ ] Energy drinks with electrolytes
- [ ] Protein-packed snacks
- [ ] Salty, easy-to-digest snacks
- [ ] Dehydrated food
- [ ] No-cook food items
- [ ] ....
- [ ] ....
- [ ] ....
- [ ] ....
- [ ] ....
- [ ] ....
- [ ] ....
- [ ] ....
- [ ] ....
- [ ] ....
- [ ] ....
- [ ] ....
- [ ] ....
- [ ] ....
- [ ] ....
- [ ] ....

PARK-SPECIFIC

- [ ] *The National Parks Journal*!
- [ ] Permits
- [ ] Guidebooks
- [ ] Park map
- [ ] ....
- [ ] ....
- [ ] ....
- [ ] ....
- [ ] ....
- [ ] ....
- [ ] ....

MISCELLANEOUS

- [ ] Duct tape
- [ ] Multipurpose tool
- [ ] Knife
- [ ] Scissors
- [ ] Can opener
- [ ] Matches/lighter/ firestarter
- [ ] Hatchet
- [ ] Whistle
- [ ] Bandana
- [ ] Quick-dry towels
- [ ] Waterproof bags
- [ ] Ziplock bags
- [ ] Trash bags
- [ ] Paper towels
- [ ] Bear can
- [ ] Binoculars
- [ ] Deck of cards/games
- [ ] Driver's license, registration, insurance, etc.
- [ ] Spare tire/jack
- [ ] Wiper blades
- [ ] Small amount of cash
- [ ] ....
- [ ] ....
- [ ] ....
- [ ] ....
- [ ] ....
- [ ] ....
- [ ] ....
- [ ] ....
- [ ] ....
- [ ] ....
- [ ] ....
- [ ] ....
- [ ] ....
- [ ] ....
- [ ] ....
- [ ] ....

PERSONALIZED LIST

- [ ] ....
- [ ] ....
- [ ] ....
- [ ] ....
- [ ] ....
- [ ] ....
- [ ] ....
- [ ] ....
- [ ] ....
- [ ] ....

TO BUY

- [ ] ....
- [ ] ....
- [ ] ....
- [ ] ....
- [ ] ....
- [ ] ....
- [ ] ....
- [ ] ....
- [ ] ....
- [ ] ....

ADDITIONAL NOTES

RECORD YOUR TRIP!

Park name: ....

State/territory: ....

Dates visited: ....

Nearby sites visited: ....

ARROWHEAD RATING!

- 5 — Epic & life-changing experience
- 4 — Want to learn everything about this park!
- 3 — See why this place is so special
- 2 — Happy I went and had some good times
- 1 — Once and done!

FAVORITE CAMPSITE OR LODGING: ....

....

PEAK EXPERIENCE: ....

....

FAVORITE ADVENTURE: ....

....

FAVORITE LOCATION: ....

....

FAVORITE PHOTO: ....

....

BEST WILDLIFE SIGHTING: ....

....

FUN THING(S) I LEARNED ABOUT THE PARK: ....

....

INTERESTING PEOPLE MET ALONG MY JOURNEY: --

VALUABLE RESOURCE(S) DISCOVERED ALONG THE WAY: --

FOOD I COULDN'T LIVE WITHOUT: --

THE BIGGEST CHALLENGE I FACED: ---

I WAS MOST PREPARED WHEN: ---

WISH I KNEW BEFORE I WENT: --

WISH I WOULD HAVE BROUGHT: --

MOST USEFUL PIECE OF GEAR: --

MOST VALUABLE TOOL: ---

MOST USEFUL PIECE OF ADVICE: --

TIPS FOR OTHER TRAVELERS: ---

ADDITIONAL NOTES: ---

PLAN YOUR TRIP!

Park name: ....

State/territory: .... Temperature range: ....

Planned dates: .... Altitude range: ....

Time zone: .... Latitude/longitude: ....

COMMITMENT LEVEL

- 6 — Full throttle, all-in adventure time!
- 5 — Bring on a big challenge!
- 4 — Many trails, sites, & adventures planned!
- 3 — Rolling where the wind blows me!
- 2 — Tons to do without breaking a big sweat!
- 1 — Easy-going, leisurely days...

SEASON OF VISIT
- ☐ Spring
- ☐ Summer
- ☐ Autumn
- ☐ Winter

TOURING/SUPPORT
- ☐ Self-guided
- ☐ Privately guided
- ☐ Chartered trip
- ☐ Group trip
- ☐ Volunteering
- ☐ Ranger-led tours
- ☐ Instructional classes
- ☐ Special events
- ....
- ....
- ....
- ....
- ....

PARK TRANSPORT
- ☐ Car
- ☐ Bus
- ☐ RV/travel trailer
- ☐ Boat
- ☐ Float plane/bush plane
- ☐ Helicopter
- ☐ Tour bus
- ☐ All-terrain vehicle
- ☐ ....

PARK ITEMS TO PICK UP
- ☐ NPS annual pass
- ☐ NPS parks passport
- ☐ Pins, patches, & stickers
- ☐ Hiking stick medallions
- ☐ NPS maps & literature
- ☐ ....
- ☐ ....
- ☐ ....

RESOURCES/CONTACTS
- ☐ NPS visitor center(s):
- ....
- ☐ Wilderness permit(s):
- ....
- ☐ Tour company:
- ....
- ☐ Local guide(s):
- ....
- ☐ Local gear outfitter(s):
- ....
- ☐ Emergency services:
- ....
- ☐ Miscellaneous contact:
- ....
- ☐ Miscellaneous contact:
- ....

MAIN ACCOMMODATIONS
- ☐ NPS lodge
- ☐ Hotel
- ☐ RV/travel trailer
- ☐ Tent camping
- ☐ Backcountry camping
- ☐ Staying with friends
- ☐ Houseboat
- ☐ Cruise ship
- ☐ Van/car
- ☐ ....
- ☐ ....

AMENITIES

- [ ] Campgrounds
  - [ ] Standard
  - [ ] RV
  - [ ] Primitive
  - [ ] Day use only
  - [ ] Group
- [ ] Plumbed bathrooms
- [ ] Showers
- [ ] Park store
- [ ] Wi-Fi
- [ ] NPS amphitheater
- [ ] Pet-friendly
- [ ] ----------------------------------
- [ ] ----------------------------------

IN-TOW

- [ ] Spouse/partner
- [ ] Children
- [ ] Pets
- [ ] Friends
- [ ] Extended family
- [ ] Boatloads of gear!
- [ ] ----------------------------------
- [ ] ----------------------------------

ADVANCED PLANNING

- [ ] Physical training?

- [ ] Seasonal aspects?

- [ ] Obtained permits?

- [ ] Purchased gear?

FINAL SAFETY CHECKS

- [ ] Left your trip plan with an emergency contact back home?
- [ ] Reviewed basic emergency aid procedures?
- [ ] Additional forms/permits needed?
- [ ] Checked on closures/mandates that might affect your travel?
- [ ] ----------------------------------
- [ ] ----------------------------------
- [ ] ----------------------------------

MAIN GOALS

- [ ] Solitude
- [ ] Active adventure
- [ ] Creative pursuits
- [ ] Learning
- [ ] Endurance training
- [ ] Gathering loved ones
- [ ] Seeing new things!
- [ ] ----------------------------------
- [ ] ----------------------------------
- [ ] ----------------------------------

IMMERSIVE EXPERIENCES

- [ ] Cultural/historical
- [ ] Volunteering
- [ ] Park programs
- [ ] Junior Ranger program
- [ ] NPS-guided night walks
- [ ] School/youth trips
- [ ] Teacher/educator programs
- [ ] Professional development
- [ ] ----------------------------------
- [ ] ----------------------------------
- [ ] ----------------------------------

ADVENTURE GOALS

- [ ] Hiking big trails
- [ ] Easy day hikes
- [ ] Cycling/mountain biking/fat biking
- [ ] Kayaking/canoeing/SUP
- [ ] Trail running
- [ ] Rafting
- [ ] Swimming
- [ ] Backpacking
- [ ] Wildlife viewing
- [ ] Scenic drives
- [ ] Fishing/angling
- [ ] Mountaineering
- [ ] Climbing/bouldering
- [ ] Photography
- [ ] Birdwatching
- [ ] Stargazing
- [ ] Cultural immersion
- [ ] Endurance training
- [ ] Picnicking
- [ ] ----------------------------------

PHOTOGRAPHY PLANS

- [ ] Wildlife
- [ ] Birds
- [ ] Landscapes
- [ ] Night skies
- [ ] People
- [ ] Cultural artifacts
- [ ] Macro/abstract
- [ ] Family pictures
- [ ] Selfies
- [ ] ----------------------------------

ADDITIONAL NOTES

PACK FOR YOUR TRIP!

Park name: ....

HEALTH & PERSONAL ITEMS

- [ ] Premade first aid kit
- [ ] Wildlife/insect protection
- [ ] Medications
- [ ] ....
- [ ] ....
- [ ] Supplements
- [ ] ....
- [ ] ....
- [ ] Eyeglasses/contacts
- [ ] Sun/wind/snow protection (eyes/skin/face)
- [ ] Facial tissues
- [ ] Bug spray
- [ ] Antibacterial wipes
- [ ] ....
- [ ] ....

ELECTRONICS

- [ ] Camera
  - [ ] Tripod
  - [ ] Lenses/lens cloths
  - [ ] Memory cards
  - [ ] Batteries & charger
- [ ] Weather protection
- [ ] External charging device
- [ ] Phone & charging cord
- [ ] Mobile Wi-Fi device
- [ ] Electronic tablet
- [ ] Satellite phone
- [ ] Personal locater beacon
- [ ] ....

CLOTHING/SHOES

- [ ] Insulated jacket
- [ ] Rain jacket/pants
- [ ] Thermal layers
- [ ] Wicked/quick-dry clothing
- [ ] Loose-fitting shirts
- [ ] Loose-fitting pants
- [ ] Hiking pants/shorts
- [ ] Short-sleeved/sleeveless shirts
- [ ] Full winter gear
- [ ] ....
- [ ] ....
- [ ] ....
- [ ] Leisurewear
- [ ] Beachwear
- [ ] Hiking shoes
- [ ] Athletic shoes
- [ ] Water shoes
- [ ] Sandals/flip-flops
- [ ] Neck gaiter
- [ ] Sun hat/cap
- [ ] Stocking cap
- [ ] Socks + extra pair
- [ ] Undergarments
- [ ] Gloves/mittens
- [ ] ....
- [ ] ....
- [ ] ....
- [ ] ....
- [ ] ....
- [ ] ....
- [ ] ....
- [ ] ....

OUTDOOR GEAR

- [ ] Hiking poles
- [ ] Tent
- [ ] Sleeping bag
- [ ] Sleeping pad
- [ ] Pillow
- [ ] Shade tent
- [ ] Emergency space blanket
- [ ] Tarp
- [ ] Daypack
- [ ] Headlamp(s)
- [ ] Lantern(s)
- [ ] Water filter & iodine tablets
- [ ] Large refillable water jug
- [ ] Portable stove
- [ ] Hot beverage thermos
- [ ] Nylon hammock
- [ ] Throw blanket
- [ ] Reusable dishes/cutlery
- [ ] Hand warmers
- [ ] ....
- [ ] ....
- [ ] ....
- [ ] ....
- [ ] ....
- [ ] ....
- [ ] ....
- [ ] ....
- [ ] ....

FOOD & DRINK

- [ ] Water
- [ ] Refillable water bottle
- [ ] Energy drinks with electrolytes
- [ ] Protein-packed snacks
- [ ] Salty, easy-to-digest snacks
- [ ] Dehydrated food
- [ ] No-cook food items
- [ ] ....
- [ ] ....
- [ ] ....
- [ ] ....
- [ ] ....
- [ ] ....
- [ ] ....
- [ ] ....
- [ ] ....
- [ ] ....
- [ ] ....
- [ ] ....
- [ ] ....
- [ ] ....

PARK-SPECIFIC

- [ ] *The National Parks Journal*!
- [ ] Permits
- [ ] Guidebooks
- [ ] Park map
- [ ] ....
- [ ] ....
- [ ] ....
- [ ] ....
- [ ] ....
- [ ] ....

MISCELLANEOUS

- [ ] Duct tape
- [ ] Multipurpose tool
- [ ] Knife
- [ ] Scissors
- [ ] Can opener
- [ ] Matches/lighter/firestarter
- [ ] Hatchet
- [ ] Whistle
- [ ] Bandana
- [ ] Quick-dry towels
- [ ] Waterproof bags
- [ ] Ziplock bags
- [ ] Trash bags
- [ ] Paper towels
- [ ] Bear can
- [ ] Binoculars
- [ ] Deck of cards/games
- [ ] Driver's license, registration, insurance, etc.
- [ ] Spare tire/jack
- [ ] Wiper blades
- [ ] Small amount of cash
- [ ] ....
- [ ] ....
- [ ] ....
- [ ] ....
- [ ] ....
- [ ] ....
- [ ] ....
- [ ] ....
- [ ] ....
- [ ] ....
- [ ] ....
- [ ] ....
- [ ] ....

PERSONALIZED LIST

- [ ] ....
- [ ] ....
- [ ] ....
- [ ] ....
- [ ] ....
- [ ] ....
- [ ] ....
- [ ] ....
- [ ] ....
- [ ] ....

TO BUY

- [ ] ....
- [ ] ....
- [ ] ....
- [ ] ....
- [ ] ....
- [ ] ....
- [ ] ....
- [ ] ....
- [ ] ....
- [ ] ....

ADDITIONAL NOTES

RECORD YOUR TRIP!

Park name: ....

State/territory: ....

Dates visited: ....

Nearby sites visited: ....

ARROWHEAD RATING!

- 5 — Epic & life-changing experience
- 4 — Want to learn everything about this park!
- 3 — See why this place is so special
- 2 — Happy I went and had some good times
- 1 — Once and done!

FAVORITE CAMPSITE OR LODGING: ....

....

PEAK EXPERIENCE: ....

....

FAVORITE ADVENTURE: ....

....

FAVORITE LOCATION: ....

....

FAVORITE PHOTO: ....

....

BEST WILDLIFE SIGHTING: ....

....

FUN THING(S) I LEARNED ABOUT THE PARK: ....

....

INTERESTING PEOPLE MET ALONG MY JOURNEY: --

VALUABLE RESOURCE(S) DISCOVERED ALONG THE WAY: ---

FOOD I COULDN'T LIVE WITHOUT: --

THE BIGGEST CHALLENGE I FACED: ---

I WAS MOST PREPARED WHEN: ---

WISH I KNEW BEFORE I WENT: --

WISH I WOULD HAVE BROUGHT: --

MOST USEFUL PIECE OF GEAR: --

MOST VALUABLE TOOL: --

MOST USEFUL PIECE OF ADVICE: ---

TIPS FOR OTHER TRAVELERS: --

ADDITIONAL NOTES: --

PLAN YOUR TRIP!

Park name: ....

State/territory: .... Temperature range: ....

Planned dates: .... Altitude range: ....

Time zone: .... Latitude/longitude: ....

COMMITMENT LEVEL

- 🛡 6 — Full throttle, all-in adventure time!
- 🛡 5 — Bring on a big challenge!
- 🛡 4 — Many trails, sites, & adventures planned!
- 🛡 3 — Rolling where the wind blows me!
- 🛡 2 — Tons to do without breaking a big sweat!
- 🛡 1 — Easy-going, leisurely days...

SEASON OF VISIT
- ☐ Spring
- ☐ Summer
- ☐ Autumn
- ☐ Winter

TOURING/SUPPORT
- ☐ Self-guided
- ☐ Privately guided
- ☐ Chartered trip
- ☐ Group trip
- ☐ Volunteering
- ☐ Ranger-led tours
- ☐ Instructional classes
- ☐ Special events
- ....
- ....
- ....
- ....
- ....

PARK TRANSPORT
- ☐ Car
- ☐ Bus
- ☐ RV/travel trailer
- ☐ Boat
- ☐ Float plane/bush plane
- ☐ Helicopter
- ☐ Tour bus
- ☐ All-terrain vehicle
- ☐ ....

PARK ITEMS TO PICK UP
- ☐ NPS annual pass
- ☐ NPS parks passport
- ☐ Pins, patches, & stickers
- ☐ Hiking stick medallions
- ☐ NPS maps & literature
- ☐ ....
- ☐ ....
- ☐ ....

RESOURCES/CONTACTS
- ☐ NPS visitor center(s):
  ....
- ☐ Wilderness permit(s):
  ....
- ☐ Tour company:
  ....
- ☐ Local guide(s):
  ....
- ☐ Local gear outfitter(s):
  ....
- ☐ Emergency services:
  ....
- ☐ Miscellaneous contact:
  ....
- ☐ Miscellaneous contact:
  ....

MAIN ACCOMMODATIONS
- ☐ NPS lodge
- ☐ Hotel
- ☐ RV/travel trailer
- ☐ Tent camping
- ☐ Backcountry camping
- ☐ Staying with friends
- ☐ Houseboat
- ☐ Cruise ship
- ☐ Van/car
- ☐ ....
- ☐ ....

AMENITIES

- [ ] Campgrounds
  - [ ] Standard
  - [ ] RV
  - [ ] Primitive
  - [ ] Day use only
  - [ ] Group
- [ ] Plumbed bathrooms
- [ ] Showers
- [ ] Park store
- [ ] Wi-Fi
- [ ] NPS amphitheater
- [ ] Pet-friendly
- [ ] ....
- [ ] ....

IN-TOW

- [ ] Spouse/partner
- [ ] Children
- [ ] Pets
- [ ] Friends
- [ ] Extended family
- [ ] Boatloads of gear!
- [ ] ....
- [ ] ....

ADVANCED PLANNING

- [ ] Physical training?

  ....
  ....

- [ ] Seasonal aspects?

  ....
  ....

- [ ] Obtained permits?

  ....
  ....

- [ ] Purchased gear?

  ....
  ....
  ....

FINAL SAFETY CHECKS

- [ ] Left your trip plan with an emergency contact back home?
- [ ] Reviewed basic emergency aid procedures?
- [ ] Additional forms/permits needed?
- [ ] Checked on closures/mandates that might affect your travel?
- [ ] ....
- [ ] ....
- [ ] ....

MAIN GOALS

- [ ] Solitude
- [ ] Active adventure
- [ ] Creative pursuits
- [ ] Learning
- [ ] Endurance training
- [ ] Gathering loved ones
- [ ] Seeing new things!
- [ ] ....
- [ ] ....
- [ ] ....

IMMERSIVE EXPERIENCES

- [ ] Cultural/historical
- [ ] Volunteering
- [ ] Park programs
- [ ] Junior Ranger program
- [ ] NPS-guided night walks
- [ ] School/youth trips
- [ ] Teacher/educator programs
- [ ] Professional development
- [ ] ....
- [ ] ....
- [ ] ....

ADVENTURE GOALS

- [ ] Hiking big trails
- [ ] Easy day hikes
- [ ] Cycling/mountain biking/fat biking
- [ ] Kayaking/canoeing/SUP
- [ ] Trail running
- [ ] Rafting
- [ ] Swimming
- [ ] Backpacking
- [ ] Wildlife viewing
- [ ] Scenic drives
- [ ] Fishing/angling
- [ ] Mountaineering
- [ ] Climbing/bouldering
- [ ] Photography
- [ ] Birdwatching
- [ ] Stargazing
- [ ] Cultural immersion
- [ ] Endurance training
- [ ] Picnicking
- [ ] ....

PHOTOGRAPHY PLANS

- [ ] Wildlife
- [ ] Birds
- [ ] Landscapes
- [ ] Night skies
- [ ] People
- [ ] Cultural artifacts
- [ ] Macro/abstract
- [ ] Family pictures
- [ ] Selfies
- [ ] ....

ADDITIONAL NOTES

....
....
....
....

PACK FOR YOUR TRIP!

Park name: ....

HEALTH & PERSONAL ITEMS

- [ ] Premade first aid kit
- [ ] Wildlife/insect protection
- [ ] Medications
- [ ] ....
- [ ] ....
- [ ] Supplements
- [ ] ....
- [ ] ....
- [ ] Eyeglasses/contacts
- [ ] Sun/wind/snow protection (eyes/skin/face)
- [ ] Facial tissues
- [ ] Bug spray
- [ ] Antibacterial wipes
- [ ] ....
- [ ] ....

ELECTRONICS

- [ ] Camera
  - [ ] Tripod
  - [ ] Lenses/lens cloths
  - [ ] Memory cards
  - [ ] Batteries & charger
- [ ] Weather protection
- [ ] External charging device
- [ ] Phone & charging cord
- [ ] Mobile Wi-Fi device
- [ ] Electronic tablet
- [ ] Satellite phone
- [ ] Personal locater beacon
- [ ] ....

CLOTHING/SHOES

- [ ] Insulated jacket
- [ ] Rain jacket/pants
- [ ] Thermal layers
- [ ] Wicked/quick-dry clothing
- [ ] Loose-fitting shirts
- [ ] Loose-fitting pants
- [ ] Hiking pants/shorts
- [ ] Short-sleeved/sleeveless shirts
- [ ] Full winter gear
- [ ] ....
- [ ] ....
- [ ] ....
- [ ] Leisurewear
- [ ] Beachwear
- [ ] Hiking shoes
- [ ] Athletic shoes
- [ ] Water shoes
- [ ] Sandals/flip-flops
- [ ] Neck gaiter
- [ ] Sun hat/cap
- [ ] Stocking cap
- [ ] Socks + extra pair
- [ ] Undergarments
- [ ] Gloves/mittens
- [ ] ....
- [ ] ....
- [ ] ....
- [ ] ....
- [ ] ....
- [ ] ....
- [ ] ....

OUTDOOR GEAR

- [ ] Hiking poles
- [ ] Tent
- [ ] Sleeping bag
- [ ] Sleeping pad
- [ ] Pillow
- [ ] Shade tent
- [ ] Emergency space blanket
- [ ] Tarp
- [ ] Daypack
- [ ] Headlamp(s)
- [ ] Lantern(s)
- [ ] Water filter & iodine tablets
- [ ] Large refillable water jug
- [ ] Portable stove
- [ ] Hot beverage thermos
- [ ] Nylon hammock
- [ ] Throw blanket
- [ ] Reusable dishes/cutlery
- [ ] Hand warmers
- [ ] ....
- [ ] ....
- [ ] ....
- [ ] ....
- [ ] ....
- [ ] ....
- [ ] ....
- [ ] ....
- [ ] ....
- [ ] ....

FOOD & DRINK

- [ ] Water
- [ ] Refillable water bottle
- [ ] Energy drinks with electrolytes
- [ ] Protein-packed snacks
- [ ] Salty, easy-to-digest snacks
- [ ] Dehydrated food
- [ ] No-cook food items
- [ ] ....
- [ ] ....
- [ ] ....
- [ ] ....
- [ ] ....
- [ ] ....
- [ ] ....
- [ ] ....
- [ ] ....
- [ ] ....
- [ ] ....
- [ ] ....
- [ ] ....
- [ ] ....
- [ ] ....
- [ ] ....
- [ ] ....

PARK-SPECIFIC

- [ ] *The National Parks Journal*!
- [ ] Permits
- [ ] Guidebooks
- [ ] Park map
- [ ] ....
- [ ] ....
- [ ] ....
- [ ] ....
- [ ] ....
- [ ] ....
- [ ]

MISCELLANEOUS

- [ ] Duct tape
- [ ] Multipurpose tool
- [ ] Knife
- [ ] Scissors
- [ ] Can opener
- [ ] Matches/lighter/ firestarter
- [ ] Hatchet
- [ ] Whistle
- [ ] Bandana
- [ ] Quick-dry towels
- [ ] Waterproof bags
- [ ] Ziplock bags
- [ ] Trash bags
- [ ] Paper towels
- [ ] Bear can
- [ ] Binoculars
- [ ] Deck of cards/games
- [ ] Driver's license, registration, insurance, etc.
- [ ] Spare tire/jack
- [ ] Wiper blades
- [ ] Small amount of cash
- [ ] ....
- [ ] ....
- [ ] ....
- [ ] ....
- [ ] ....
- [ ] ....
- [ ] ....
- [ ] ....
- [ ] ....
- [ ] ....
- [ ] ....
- [ ] ....
- [ ] ....
- [ ] ....
- [ ] ....
- [ ] ....

PERSONALIZED LIST

- [ ] ....
- [ ] ....
- [ ] ....
- [ ] ....
- [ ] ....
- [ ] ....
- [ ] ....
- [ ] ....
- [ ] ....
- [ ] ....

TO BUY

- [ ] ....
- [ ] ....
- [ ] ....
- [ ] ....
- [ ] ....
- [ ] ....
- [ ] ....
- [ ] ....
- [ ] ....
- [ ] ....

ADDITIONAL NOTES

....
....
....
....
....
....
....
....
....
....
....
....
....
....

RECORD YOUR TRIP!

Park name: ....

State/territory: ....

Dates visited: ....

Nearby sites visited: ....

- 5 — Epic & life-changing experience
- 4 — Want to learn everything about this park!
- 3 — See why this place is so special
- 2 — Happy I went and had some good times
- 1 — Once and done!

FAVORITE CAMPSITE OR LODGING: ....

....

PEAK EXPERIENCE: ....

....

FAVORITE ADVENTURE: ....

....

FAVORITE LOCATION: ....

....

FAVORITE PHOTO: ....

....

BEST WILDLIFE SIGHTING: ....

....

FUN THING(S) I LEARNED ABOUT THE PARK: ....

....

INTERESTING PEOPLE MET ALONG MY JOURNEY:

VALUABLE RESOURCE(S) DISCOVERED ALONG THE WAY:

FOOD I COULDN'T LIVE WITHOUT:

THE BIGGEST CHALLENGE I FACED:

I WAS MOST PREPARED WHEN:

WISH I KNEW BEFORE I WENT:

WISH I WOULD HAVE BROUGHT:

MOST USEFUL PIECE OF GEAR:

MOST VALUABLE TOOL:

MOST USEFUL PIECE OF ADVICE:

TIPS FOR OTHER TRAVELERS:

ADDITIONAL NOTES:

PLAN YOUR TRIP!

Park name: ....

State/territory: ....   Temperature range: ....

Planned dates: ....   Altitude range: ....

Time zone: ....   Latitude/longitude: ....

COMMITMENT LEVEL

6 — Full throttle, all-in adventure time!

5 — Bring on a big challenge!

4 — Many trails, sites, & adventures planned!

3 — Rolling where the wind blows me!

2 — Tons to do without breaking a big sweat!

1 — Easy-going, leisurely days...

SEASON OF VISIT

☐ Spring
☐ Summer
☐ Autumn
☐ Winter

TOURING/SUPPORT

☐ Self-guided
☐ Privately guided
☐ Chartered trip
☐ Group trip
☐ Volunteering
☐ Ranger-led tours
☐ Instructional classes
☐ Special events

PARK TRANSPORT

☐ Car
☐ Bus
☐ RV/travel trailer
☐ Boat
☐ Float plane/bush plane
☐ Helicopter
☐ Tour bus
☐ All-terrain vehicle
☐ ---------------------

PARK ITEMS TO PICK UP

☐ NPS annual pass
☐ NPS parks passport
☐ Pins, patches, & stickers
☐ Hiking stick medallions
☐ NPS maps & literature
☐ ---------------------
☐ ---------------------
☐ ---------------------

RESOURCES/CONTACTS

☐ NPS visitor center(s):

☐ Wilderness permit(s):

☐ Tour company:

☐ Local guide(s):

☐ Local gear outfitter(s):

☐ Emergency services:

☐ Miscellaneous contact:

☐ Miscellaneous contact:

MAIN ACCOMMODATIONS

☐ NPS lodge
☐ Hotel
☐ RV/travel trailer
☐ Tent camping
☐ Backcountry camping
☐ Staying with friends
☐ Houseboat
☐ Cruise ship
☐ Van/car
☐ ---------------------
☐ ---------------------

AMENITIES

- [ ] Campgrounds
  - [ ] Standard
  - [ ] RV
  - [ ] Primitive
  - [ ] Day use only
  - [ ] Group
- [ ] Plumbed bathrooms
- [ ] Showers
- [ ] Park store
- [ ] Wi-Fi
- [ ] NPS amphitheater
- [ ] Pet-friendly
- [ ] ....
- [ ] ....

IN-TOW

- [ ] Spouse/partner
- [ ] Children
- [ ] Pets
- [ ] Friends
- [ ] Extended family
- [ ] Boatloads of gear!
- [ ] ....
- [ ] ....

ADVANCED PLANNING

- [ ] Physical training?

  ....
  ....
- [ ] Seasonal aspects?

  ....
  ....
- [ ] Obtained permits?

  ....
  ....
- [ ] Purchased gear?

  ....
  ....
  ....

FINAL SAFETY CHECKS

- [ ] Left your trip plan with an emergency contact back home?
- [ ] Reviewed basic emergency aid procedures?
- [ ] Additional forms/permits needed?
- [ ] Checked on closures/mandates that might affect your travel?
- [ ] ....
- [ ] ....
- [ ] ....

MAIN GOALS

- [ ] Solitude
- [ ] Active adventure
- [ ] Creative pursuits
- [ ] Learning
- [ ] Endurance training
- [ ] Gathering loved ones
- [ ] Seeing new things!
- [ ] ....
- [ ] ....
- [ ] ....

IMMERSIVE EXPERIENCES

- [ ] Cultural/historical
- [ ] Volunteering
- [ ] Park programs
- [ ] Junior Ranger program
- [ ] NPS-guided night walks
- [ ] School/youth trips
- [ ] Teacher/educator programs
- [ ] Professional development
- [ ] ....
- [ ] ....
- [ ] ....

ADVENTURE GOALS

- [ ] Hiking big trails
- [ ] Easy day hikes
- [ ] Cycling/mountain biking/fat biking
- [ ] Kayaking/canoeing/SUP
- [ ] Trail running
- [ ] Rafting
- [ ] Swimming
- [ ] Backpacking
- [ ] Wildlife viewing
- [ ] Scenic drives
- [ ] Fishing/angling
- [ ] Mountaineering
- [ ] Climbing/bouldering
- [ ] Photography
- [ ] Birdwatching
- [ ] Stargazing
- [ ] Cultural immersion
- [ ] Endurance training
- [ ] Picnicking
- [ ] ....

PHOTOGRAPHY PLANS

- [ ] Wildlife
- [ ] Birds
- [ ] Landscapes
- [ ] Night skies
- [ ] People
- [ ] Cultural artifacts
- [ ] Macro/abstract
- [ ] Family pictures
- [ ] Selfies
- [ ] ....

ADDITIONAL NOTES

....
....
....
....
....

PACK FOR YOUR TRIP!

Park name: ....

- ☐ Premade first aid kit
- ☐ Wildlife/insect protection
- ☐ Medications
- ☐ ....
- ☐ ....
- ☐ Supplements
- ☐ ....
- ☐ ....
- ☐ Eyeglasses/contacts
- ☐ Sun/wind/snow protection (eyes/skin/face)
- ☐ Facial tissues
- ☐ Bug spray
- ☐ Antibacterial wipes
- ☐ ....
- ☐ ....

ELECTRONICS

- ☐ Camera
  - ☐ Tripod
  - ☐ Lenses/lens cloths
  - ☐ Memory cards
  - ☐ Batteries & charger
- ☐ Weather protection
- ☐ External charging device
- ☐ Phone & charging cord
- ☐ Mobile Wi-Fi device
- ☐ Electronic tablet
- ☐ Satellite phone
- ☐ Personal locater beacon
- ☐ ....

CLOTHING/SHOES

- ☐ Insulated jacket
- ☐ Rain jacket/pants
- ☐ Thermal layers
- ☐ Wicked/quick-dry clothing
- ☐ Loose-fitting shirts
- ☐ Loose-fitting pants
- ☐ Hiking pants/shorts
- ☐ Short-sleeved/sleeveless shirts
- ☐ Full winter gear
- ☐ ....
- ☐ ....
- ☐ ....
- ☐ Leisurewear
- ☐ Beachwear
- ☐ Hiking shoes
- ☐ Athletic shoes
- ☐ Water shoes
- ☐ Sandals/flip-flops
- ☐ Neck gaiter
- ☐ Sun hat/cap
- ☐ Stocking cap
- ☐ Socks + extra pair
- ☐ Undergarments
- ☐ Gloves/mittens
- ☐ ....
- ☐ ....
- ☐ ....
- ☐ ....
- ☐ ....
- ☐ ....
- ☐ ....

OUTDOOR GEAR

- ☐ Hiking poles
- ☐ Tent
- ☐ Sleeping bag
- ☐ Sleeping pad
- ☐ Pillow
- ☐ Shade tent
- ☐ Emergency space blanket
- ☐ Tarp
- ☐ Daypack
- ☐ Headlamp(s)
- ☐ Lantern(s)
- ☐ Water filter & iodine tablets
- ☐ Large refillable water jug
- ☐ Portable stove
- ☐ Hot beverage thermos
- ☐ Nylon hammock
- ☐ Throw blanket
- ☐ Reusable dishes/cutlery
- ☐ Hand warmers
- ☐ ....
- ☐ ....
- ☐ ....
- ☐ ....
- ☐ ....
- ☐ ....
- ☐ ....
- ☐ ....
- ☐ ....
- ☐ ....

FOOD & DRINK

- [ ] Water
- [ ] Refillable water bottle
- [ ] Energy drinks with electrolytes
- [ ] Protein-packed snacks
- [ ] Salty, easy-to-digest snacks
- [ ] Dehydrated food
- [ ] No-cook food items
- [ ] ....
- [ ] ....
- [ ] ....
- [ ] ....
- [ ] ....
- [ ] ....
- [ ] ....
- [ ] ....
- [ ] ....
- [ ] ....
- [ ] ....
- [ ] ....
- [ ] ....
- [ ] ....
- [ ] ....

PARK-SPECIFIC

- [ ] *The National Parks Journal*!
- [ ] Permits
- [ ] Guidebooks
- [ ] Park map
- [ ] ....
- [ ] ....
- [ ] ....
- [ ] ....
- [ ] ....
- [ ] ....

MISCELLANEOUS

- [ ] Duct tape
- [ ] Multipurpose tool
- [ ] Knife
- [ ] Scissors
- [ ] Can opener
- [ ] Matches/lighter/ firestarter
- [ ] Hatchet
- [ ] Whistle
- [ ] Bandana
- [ ] Quick-dry towels
- [ ] Waterproof bags
- [ ] Ziplock bags
- [ ] Trash bags
- [ ] Paper towels
- [ ] Bear can
- [ ] Binoculars
- [ ] Deck of cards/games
- [ ] Driver's license, registration, insurance, etc.
- [ ] Spare tire/jack
- [ ] Wiper blades
- [ ] Small amount of cash
- [ ] ....
- [ ] ....
- [ ] ....
- [ ] ....
- [ ] ....
- [ ] ....
- [ ] ....
- [ ] ....
- [ ] ....
- [ ] ....
- [ ] ....
- [ ] ....
- [ ] ....
- [ ] ....

PERSONALIZED LIST

- [ ] ....
- [ ] ....
- [ ] ....
- [ ] ....
- [ ] ....
- [ ] ....
- [ ] ....
- [ ] ....
- [ ] ....
- [ ] ....
- [ ] ....
- [ ] ....

TO BUY

- [ ] ....
- [ ] ....
- [ ] ....
- [ ] ....
- [ ] ....
- [ ] ....
- [ ] ....
- [ ] ....
- [ ] ....
- [ ] ....

ADDITIONAL NOTES

RECORD YOUR TRIP!

Park name: ....

State/territory: ....

Dates visited: ....

Nearby sites visited: ....

ARROWHEAD RATING!

5 — Epic & life-changing experience

4 — Want to learn everything about this park!

3 — See why this place is so special

2 — Happy I went and had some good times

1 — Once and done!

FAVORITE CAMPSITE OR LODGING: ....

....

PEAK EXPERIENCE: ....

....

FAVORITE ADVENTURE: ....

....

FAVORITE LOCATION: ....

....

FAVORITE PHOTO: ....

....

BEST WILDLIFE SIGHTING: ....

....

FUN THING(S) I LEARNED ABOUT THE PARK: ....

....

INTERESTING PEOPLE MET ALONG MY JOURNEY: --

VALUABLE RESOURCE(S) DISCOVERED ALONG THE WAY: -----------------------------

----

FOOD I COULDN'T LIVE WITHOUT: ---

THE BIGGEST CHALLENGE I FACED: --

I WAS MOST PREPARED WHEN: ---

WISH I KNEW BEFORE I WENT: --

WISH I WOULD HAVE BROUGHT: --

MOST USEFUL PIECE OF GEAR: --

MOST VALUABLE TOOL: ---

MOST USEFUL PIECE OF ADVICE: --

TIPS FOR OTHER TRAVELERS: ---

ADDITIONAL NOTES: ---

PLAN YOUR TRIP!

Park name: ....

State/territory: ....   Temperature range: ....

Planned dates: ....   Altitude range: ....

Time zone: ....   Latitude/longitude: ....

COMMITMENT LEVEL

- ⛨ 6 — Full throttle, all-in adventure time!
- ⛨ 5 — Bring on a big challenge!
- ⛨ 4 — Many trails, sites, & adventures planned!
- ⛨ 3 — Rolling where the wind blows me!
- ⛨ 2 — Tons to do without breaking a big sweat!
- ⛨ 1 — Easy-going, leisurely days...

SEASON OF VISIT

- ☐ Spring
- ☐ Summer
- ☐ Autumn
- ☐ Winter

TOURING/SUPPORT

- ☐ Self-guided
- ☐ Privately guided
- ☐ Chartered trip
- ☐ Group trip
- ☐ Volunteering
- ☐ Ranger-led tours
- ☐ Instructional classes
- ☐ Special events
- ....
- ....
- ....
- ....
- ....

PARK TRANSPORT

- ☐ Car
- ☐ Bus
- ☐ RV/travel trailer
- ☐ Boat
- ☐ Float plane/bush plane
- ☐ Helicopter
- ☐ Tour bus
- ☐ All-terrain vehicle
- ☐ ....

PARK ITEMS TO PICK UP

- ☐ NPS annual pass
- ☐ NPS parks passport
- ☐ Pins, patches, & stickers
- ☐ Hiking stick medallions
- ☐ NPS maps & literature
- ☐ ....
- ☐ ....
- ☐ ....

RESOURCES/CONTACTS

- ☐ NPS visitor center(s):
  ....
- ☐ Wilderness permit(s):
  ....
- ☐ Tour company:
  ....
- ☐ Local guide(s):
  ....
- ☐ Local gear outfitter(s):
  ....
- ☐ Emergency services:
  ....
- ☐ Miscellaneous contact:
  ....
- ☐ Miscellaneous contact:
  ....

MAIN ACCOMMODATIONS

- ☐ NPS lodge
- ☐ Hotel
- ☐ RV/travel trailer
- ☐ Tent camping
- ☐ Backcountry camping
- ☐ Staying with friends
- ☐ Houseboat
- ☐ Cruise ship
- ☐ Van/car
- ☐ ....
- ☐ ....

AMENITIES

- [ ] Campgrounds
  - [ ] Standard
  - [ ] RV
  - [ ] Primitive
  - [ ] Day use only
  - [ ] Group
- [ ] Plumbed bathrooms
- [ ] Showers
- [ ] Park store
- [ ] Wi-Fi
- [ ] NPS amphitheater
- [ ] Pet-friendly
- [ ] ----------------------------------
- [ ] ----------------------------------

IN-TOW

- [ ] Spouse/partner
- [ ] Children
- [ ] Pets
- [ ] Friends
- [ ] Extended family
- [ ] Boatloads of gear!
- [ ] ----------------------------------
- [ ] ----------------------------------

ADVANCED PLANNING

- [ ] Physical training?

- [ ] Seasonal aspects?

- [ ] Obtained permits?

- [ ] Purchased gear?

FINAL SAFETY CHECKS

- [ ] Left your trip plan with an emergency contact back home?
- [ ] Reviewed basic emergency aid procedures?
- [ ] Additional forms/permits needed?
- [ ] Checked on closures/mandates that might affect your travel?
- [ ] ----------------------------------
- [ ] ----------------------------------
- [ ] ----------------------------------

MAIN GOALS

- [ ] Solitude
- [ ] Active adventure
- [ ] Creative pursuits
- [ ] Learning
- [ ] Endurance training
- [ ] Gathering loved ones
- [ ] Seeing new things!
- [ ] ----------------------------------
- [ ] ----------------------------------
- [ ] ----------------------------------

IMMERSIVE EXPERIENCES

- [ ] Cultural/historical
- [ ] Volunteering
- [ ] Park programs
- [ ] Junior Ranger program
- [ ] NPS-guided night walks
- [ ] School/youth trips
- [ ] Teacher/educator programs
- [ ] Professional development
- [ ] ----------------------------------
- [ ] ----------------------------------
- [ ] ----------------------------------

ADVENTURE GOALS

- [ ] Hiking big trails
- [ ] Easy day hikes
- [ ] Cycling/mountain biking/fat biking
- [ ] Kayaking/canoeing/SUP
- [ ] Trail running
- [ ] Rafting
- [ ] Swimming
- [ ] Backpacking
- [ ] Wildlife viewing
- [ ] Scenic drives
- [ ] Fishing/angling
- [ ] Mountaineering
- [ ] Climbing/bouldering
- [ ] Photography
- [ ] Birdwatching
- [ ] Stargazing
- [ ] Cultural immersion
- [ ] Endurance training
- [ ] Picnicking
- [ ] ----------------------------------

PHOTOGRAPHY PLANS

- [ ] Wildlife
- [ ] Birds
- [ ] Landscapes
- [ ] Night skies
- [ ] People
- [ ] Cultural artifacts
- [ ] Macro/abstract
- [ ] Family pictures
- [ ] Selfies
- [ ] ----------------------------------

ADDITIONAL NOTES

PACK FOR YOUR TRIP!

Park name: ....

HEALTH & PERSONAL ITEMS

- ☐ Premade first aid kit
- ☐ Wildlife/insect protection
- ☐ Medications
- ☐ ....
- ☐ ....
- ☐ Supplements
- ☐ ....
- ☐ ....
- ☐ Eyeglasses/contacts
- ☐ Sun/wind/snow protection (eyes/skin/face)
- ☐ Facial tissues
- ☐ Bug spray
- ☐ Antibacterial wipes
- ☐ ....
- ☐ ....

ELECTRONICS

- ☐ Camera
  - ☐ Tripod
  - ☐ Lenses/lens cloths
  - ☐ Memory cards
  - ☐ Batteries & charger
- ☐ Weather protection
- ☐ External charging device
- ☐ Phone & charging cord
- ☐ Mobile Wi-Fi device
- ☐ Electronic tablet
- ☐ Satellite phone
- ☐ Personal locater beacon
- ☐ ....

CLOTHING/SHOES

- ☐ Insulated jacket
- ☐ Rain jacket/pants
- ☐ Thermal layers
- ☐ Wicked/quick-dry clothing
- ☐ Loose-fitting shirts
- ☐ Loose-fitting pants
- ☐ Hiking pants/shorts
- ☐ Short-sleeved/sleeveless shirts
- ☐ Full winter gear
- ☐ ....
- ☐ ....
- ☐ ....
- ☐ Leisurewear
- ☐ Beachwear
- ☐ Hiking shoes
- ☐ Athletic shoes
- ☐ Water shoes
- ☐ Sandals/flip-flops
- ☐ Neck gaiter
- ☐ Sun hat/cap
- ☐ Stocking cap
- ☐ Socks + extra pair
- ☐ Undergarments
- ☐ Gloves/mittens
- ☐ ....
- ☐ ....
- ☐ ....
- ☐ ....
- ☐ ....
- ☐ ....
- ☐ ....

OUTDOOR GEAR

- ☐ Hiking poles
- ☐ Tent
- ☐ Sleeping bag
- ☐ Sleeping pad
- ☐ Pillow
- ☐ Shade tent
- ☐ Emergency space blanket
- ☐ Tarp
- ☐ Daypack
- ☐ Headlamp(s)
- ☐ Lantern(s)
- ☐ Water filter & iodine tablets
- ☐ Large refillable water jug
- ☐ Portable stove
- ☐ Hot beverage thermos
- ☐ Nylon hammock
- ☐ Throw blanket
- ☐ Reusable dishes/cutlery
- ☐ Hand warmers
- ☐ ....
- ☐ ....
- ☐ ....
- ☐ ....
- ☐ ....
- ☐ ....
- ☐ ....
- ☐ ....
- ☐ ....
- ☐ ....
- ☐ ....

FOOD & DRINK

- [ ] Water
- [ ] Refillable water bottle
- [ ] Energy drinks with electrolytes
- [ ] Protein-packed snacks
- [ ] Salty, easy-to-digest snacks
- [ ] Dehydrated food
- [ ] No-cook food items
- [ ] ....
- [ ] ....
- [ ] ....
- [ ] ....
- [ ] ....
- [ ] ....
- [ ] ....
- [ ] ....
- [ ] ....
- [ ] ....
- [ ] ....
- [ ] ....
- [ ] ....
- [ ] ....
- [ ] ....

PARK-SPECIFIC

- [ ] *The National Parks Journal*!
- [ ] Permits
- [ ] Guidebooks
- [ ] Park map
- [ ] ....
- [ ] ....
- [ ] ....
- [ ] ....
- [ ] ....
- [ ] ....
- [ ] ....

MISCELLANEOUS

- [ ] Duct tape
- [ ] Multipurpose tool
- [ ] Knife
- [ ] Scissors
- [ ] Can opener
- [ ] Matches/lighter/firestarter
- [ ] Hatchet
- [ ] Whistle
- [ ] Bandana
- [ ] Quick-dry towels
- [ ] Waterproof bags
- [ ] Ziplock bags
- [ ] Trash bags
- [ ] Paper towels
- [ ] Bear can
- [ ] Binoculars
- [ ] Deck of cards/games
- [ ] Driver's license, registration, insurance, etc.
- [ ] Spare tire/jack
- [ ] Wiper blades
- [ ] Small amount of cash
- [ ] ....
- [ ] ....
- [ ] ....
- [ ] ....
- [ ] ....
- [ ] ....
- [ ] ....
- [ ] ....
- [ ] ....
- [ ] ....
- [ ] ....
- [ ] ....
- [ ] ....
- [ ] ....
- [ ] ....

PERSONALIZED LIST

- [ ] ....
- [ ] ....
- [ ] ....
- [ ] ....
- [ ] ....
- [ ] ....
- [ ] ....
- [ ] ....
- [ ] ....
- [ ] ....
- [ ] ....

TO BUY

- [ ] ....
- [ ] ....
- [ ] ....
- [ ] ....
- [ ] ....
- [ ] ....
- [ ] ....
- [ ] ....
- [ ] ....
- [ ] ....

ADDITIONAL NOTES

RECORD YOUR TRIP!

Park name: ....

State/territory: ....

Dates visited: ....

Nearby sites visited: ....

ARROWHEAD RATING!

- 5 — Epic & life-changing experience
- 4 — Want to learn everything about this park!
- 3 — See why this place is so special
- 2 — Happy I went and had some good times
- 1 — Once and done!

FAVORITE CAMPSITE OR LODGING: ....
....

PEAK EXPERIENCE: ....
....

FAVORITE ADVENTURE: ....
....

FAVORITE LOCATION: ....
....

FAVORITE PHOTO: ....
....

BEST WILDLIFE SIGHTING: ....
....

FUN THING(S) I LEARNED ABOUT THE PARK: ....
....

INTERESTING PEOPLE MET ALONG MY JOURNEY: --

VALUABLE RESOURCE(S) DISCOVERED ALONG THE WAY: --

FOOD I COULDN'T LIVE WITHOUT: ---

THE BIGGEST CHALLENGE I FACED: --

I WAS MOST PREPARED WHEN: ---

WISH I KNEW BEFORE I WENT: ---

WISH I WOULD HAVE BROUGHT: ---

MOST USEFUL PIECE OF GEAR: ---

MOST VALUABLE TOOL: --

MOST USEFUL PIECE OF ADVICE: --

TIPS FOR OTHER TRAVELERS: ---

ADDITIONAL NOTES: --

PLAN YOUR TRIP!

Park name: ....

State/territory: ....   Temperature range: ....

Planned dates: ....   Altitude range: ....

Time zone: ....   Latitude/longitude: ....

AMENITIES

- [ ] Campgrounds
  - [ ] Standard
  - [ ] RV
  - [ ] Primitive
  - [ ] Day use only
  - [ ] Group
- [ ] Plumbed bathrooms
- [ ] Showers
- [ ] Park store
- [ ] Wi-Fi
- [ ] NPS amphitheater
- [ ] Pet-friendly
- [ ] --
- [ ] --

IN-TOW

- [ ] Spouse/partner
- [ ] Children
- [ ] Pets
- [ ] Friends
- [ ] Extended family
- [ ] Boatloads of gear!
- [ ] --
- [ ] --

ADVANCED PLANNING

- [ ] Physical training?

- [ ] Seasonal aspects?

- [ ] Obtained permits?

- [ ] Purchased gear?

FINAL SAFETY CHECKS

- [ ] Left your trip plan with an emergency contact back home?
- [ ] Reviewed basic emergency aid procedures?
- [ ] Additional forms/permits needed?
- [ ] Checked on closures/mandates that might affect your travel?
- [ ] --
- [ ] --
- [ ] --

MAIN GOALS

- [ ] Solitude
- [ ] Active adventure
- [ ] Creative pursuits
- [ ] Learning
- [ ] Endurance training
- [ ] Gathering loved ones
- [ ] Seeing new things!
- [ ] --
- [ ] --
- [ ] --

IMMERSIVE EXPERIENCES

- [ ] Cultural/historical
- [ ] Volunteering
- [ ] Park programs
- [ ] Junior Ranger program
- [ ] NPS-guided night walks
- [ ] School/youth trips
- [ ] Teacher/educator programs
- [ ] Professional development
- [ ] --
- [ ] --
- [ ] --

ADVENTURE GOALS

- [ ] Hiking big trails
- [ ] Easy day hikes
- [ ] Cycling/mountain biking/fat biking
- [ ] Kayaking/canoeing/SUP
- [ ] Trail running
- [ ] Rafting
- [ ] Swimming
- [ ] Backpacking
- [ ] Wildlife viewing
- [ ] Scenic drives
- [ ] Fishing/angling
- [ ] Mountaineering
- [ ] Climbing/bouldering
- [ ] Photography
- [ ] Birdwatching
- [ ] Stargazing
- [ ] Cultural immersion
- [ ] Endurance training
- [ ] Picnicking
- [ ] --

PHOTOGRAPHY PLANS

- [ ] Wildlife
- [ ] Birds
- [ ] Landscapes
- [ ] Night skies
- [ ] People
- [ ] Cultural artifacts
- [ ] Macro/abstract
- [ ] Family pictures
- [ ] Selfies
- [ ] --

ADDITIONAL NOTES

PACK FOR YOUR TRIP!

Park name: ....

HEALTH & PERSONAL ITEMS

- [ ] Premade first aid kit
- [ ] Wildlife/insect protection
- [ ] Medications
- [ ] ....
- [ ] ....
- [ ] Supplements
- [ ] ....
- [ ] ....
- [ ] Eyeglasses/contacts
- [ ] Sun/wind/snow protection (eyes/skin/face)
- [ ] Facial tissues
- [ ] Bug spray
- [ ] Antibacterial wipes
- [ ] ....
- [ ] ....

ELECTRONICS

- [ ] Camera
  - [ ] Tripod
  - [ ] Lenses/lens cloths
  - [ ] Memory cards
  - [ ] Batteries & charger
- [ ] Weather protection
- [ ] External charging device
- [ ] Phone & charging cord
- [ ] Mobile Wi-Fi device
- [ ] Electronic tablet
- [ ] Satellite phone
- [ ] Personal locater beacon
- [ ] ....

CLOTHING/SHOES

- [ ] Insulated jacket
- [ ] Rain jacket/pants
- [ ] Thermal layers
- [ ] Wicked/quick-dry clothing
- [ ] Loose-fitting shirts
- [ ] Loose-fitting pants
- [ ] Hiking pants/shorts
- [ ] Short-sleeved/sleeveless shirts
- [ ] Full winter gear
- [ ] ....
- [ ] ....
- [ ] ....
- [ ] Leisurewear
- [ ] Beachwear
- [ ] Hiking shoes
- [ ] Athletic shoes
- [ ] Water shoes
- [ ] Sandals/flip-flops
- [ ] Neck gaiter
- [ ] Sun hat/cap
- [ ] Stocking cap
- [ ] Socks + extra pair
- [ ] Undergarments
- [ ] Gloves/mittens
- [ ] ....
- [ ] ....
- [ ] ....
- [ ] ....
- [ ] ....
- [ ] ....
- [ ] ....

OUTDOOR GEAR

- [ ] Hiking poles
- [ ] Tent
- [ ] Sleeping bag
- [ ] Sleeping pad
- [ ] Pillow
- [ ] Shade tent
- [ ] Emergency space blanket
- [ ] Tarp
- [ ] Daypack
- [ ] Headlamp(s)
- [ ] Lantern(s)
- [ ] Water filter & iodine tablets
- [ ] Large refillable water jug
- [ ] Portable stove
- [ ] Hot beverage thermos
- [ ] Nylon hammock
- [ ] Throw blanket
- [ ] Reusable dishes/cutlery
- [ ] Hand warmers
- [ ] ....
- [ ] ....
- [ ] ....
- [ ] ....
- [ ] ....
- [ ] ....
- [ ] ....
- [ ] ....
- [ ] ....
- [ ] ....

FOOD & DRINK

- [ ] Water
- [ ] Refillable water bottle
- [ ] Energy drinks with electrolytes
- [ ] Protein-packed snacks
- [ ] Salty, easy-to-digest snacks
- [ ] Dehydrated food
- [ ] No-cook food items
- [ ] ....
- [ ] ....
- [ ] ....
- [ ] ....
- [ ] ....
- [ ] ....
- [ ] ....
- [ ] ....
- [ ] ....
- [ ] ....
- [ ] ....
- [ ] ....
- [ ] ....
- [ ] ....
- [ ] ....
- [ ] ....

PARK-SPECIFIC

- [ ] *The National Parks Journal*!
- [ ] Permits
- [ ] Guidebooks
- [ ] Park map
- [ ] ....
- [ ] ....
- [ ] ....
- [ ] ....
- [ ] ....
- [ ] ....
- [ ] ....

MISCELLANEOUS

- [ ] Duct tape
- [ ] Multipurpose tool
- [ ] Knife
- [ ] Scissors
- [ ] Can opener
- [ ] Matches/lighter/firestarter
- [ ] Hatchet
- [ ] Whistle
- [ ] Bandana
- [ ] Quick-dry towels
- [ ] Waterproof bags
- [ ] Ziplock bags
- [ ] Trash bags
- [ ] Paper towels
- [ ] Bear can
- [ ] Binoculars
- [ ] Deck of cards/games
- [ ] Driver's license, registration, insurance, etc.
- [ ] Spare tire/jack
- [ ] Wiper blades
- [ ] Small amount of cash
- [ ] ....
- [ ] ....
- [ ] ....
- [ ] ....
- [ ] ....
- [ ] ....
- [ ] ....
- [ ] ....
- [ ] ....
- [ ] ....
- [ ] ....
- [ ] ....
- [ ] ....
- [ ] ....
- [ ] ....
- [ ] ....

PERSONALIZED LIST

- [ ] ....
- [ ] ....
- [ ] ....
- [ ] ....
- [ ] ....
- [ ] ....
- [ ] ....
- [ ] ....
- [ ] ....
- [ ] ....
- [ ] ....

TO BUY

- [ ] ....
- [ ] ....
- [ ] ....
- [ ] ....
- [ ] ....
- [ ] ....
- [ ] ....
- [ ] ....
- [ ] ....
- [ ] ....

ADDITIONAL NOTES

RECORD YOUR TRIP!

Park name: ....

State/territory: ....

Dates visited: ....

Nearby sites visited: ....

ARROWHEAD RATING!

5 — Epic & life-changing experience
4 — Want to learn everything about this park!
3 — See why this place is so special
2 — Happy I went and had some good times
1 — Once and done!

FAVORITE CAMPSITE OR LODGING: ....

....

PEAK EXPERIENCE: ....

....

FAVORITE ADVENTURE: ....

....

FAVORITE LOCATION: ....

....

FAVORITE PHOTO: ....

....

BEST WILDLIFE SIGHTING: ....

....

FUN THING(S) I LEARNED ABOUT THE PARK: ....

....

INTERESTING PEOPLE MET ALONG MY JOURNEY: --

VALUABLE RESOURCE(S) DISCOVERED ALONG THE WAY: -----------------------------------

----

FOOD I COULDN'T LIVE WITHOUT: --

THE BIGGEST CHALLENGE I FACED: ---

I WAS MOST PREPARED WHEN: --

WISH I KNEW BEFORE I WENT: --

WISH I WOULD HAVE BROUGHT: --

MOST USEFUL PIECE OF GEAR: --

MOST VALUABLE TOOL: --

MOST USEFUL PIECE OF ADVICE: ---

TIPS FOR OTHER TRAVELERS: ---

ADDITIONAL NOTES: ---

PLAN YOUR TRIP!

Park name: ....

State/territory: .... Temperature range: ....

Planned dates: .... Altitude range: ....

Time zone: .... Latitude/longitude: ....

COMMITMENT LEVEL

6 — Full throttle, all-in adventure time!

5 — Bring on a big challenge!

4 — Many trails, sites, & adventures planned!

3 — Rolling where the wind blows me!

2 — Tons to do without breaking a big sweat!

1 — Easy-going, leisurely days...

SEASON OF VISIT

- [ ] Spring
- [ ] Summer
- [ ] Autumn
- [ ] Winter

TOURING/SUPPORT

- [ ] Self-guided
- [ ] Privately guided
- [ ] Chartered trip
- [ ] Group trip
- [ ] Volunteering
- [ ] Ranger-led tours
- [ ] Instructional classes
- [ ] Special events
- [ ] ....
- [ ] ....
- [ ] ....
- [ ] ....

PARK TRANSPORT

- [ ] Car
- [ ] Bus
- [ ] RV/travel trailer
- [ ] Boat
- [ ] Float plane/bush plane
- [ ] Helicopter
- [ ] Tour bus
- [ ] All-terrain vehicle
- [ ] ....

PARK ITEMS TO PICK UP

- [ ] NPS annual pass
- [ ] NPS parks passport
- [ ] Pins, patches, & stickers
- [ ] Hiking stick medallions
- [ ] NPS maps & literature
- [ ] ....
- [ ] ....
- [ ] ....

RESOURCES/CONTACTS

- [ ] NPS visitor center(s):
  ....
- [ ] Wilderness permit(s):
  ....
- [ ] Tour company:
  ....
- [ ] Local guide(s):
  ....
- [ ] Local gear outfitter(s):
  ....
- [ ] Emergency services:
  ....
- [ ] Miscellaneous contact:
  ....
- [ ] Miscellaneous contact:
  ....

MAIN ACCOMMODATIONS

- [ ] NPS lodge
- [ ] Hotel
- [ ] RV/travel trailer
- [ ] Tent camping
- [ ] Backcountry camping
- [ ] Staying with friends
- [ ] Houseboat
- [ ] Cruise ship
- [ ] Van/car
- [ ] ....
- [ ] ....

AMENITIES

- [ ] Campgrounds
  - [ ] Standard
  - [ ] RV
  - [ ] Primitive
  - [ ] Day use only
  - [ ] Group
- [ ] Plumbed bathrooms
- [ ] Showers
- [ ] Park store
- [ ] Wi-Fi
- [ ] NPS amphitheater
- [ ] Pet-friendly
- [ ] ----------------------------------
- [ ] ----------------------------------

IN-TOW

- [ ] Spouse/partner
- [ ] Children
- [ ] Pets
- [ ] Friends
- [ ] Extended family
- [ ] Boatloads of gear!
- [ ] ----------------------------------
- [ ] ----------------------------------

ADVANCED PLANNING

- [ ] Physical training?

- [ ] Seasonal aspects?

- [ ] Obtained permits?

- [ ] Purchased gear?

FINAL SAFETY CHECKS

- [ ] Left your trip plan with an emergency contact back home?
- [ ] Reviewed basic emergency aid procedures?
- [ ] Additional forms/permits needed?
- [ ] Checked on closures/mandates that might affect your travel?
- [ ] ----------------------------------
- [ ] ----------------------------------
- [ ] ----------------------------------

MAIN GOALS

- [ ] Solitude
- [ ] Active adventure
- [ ] Creative pursuits
- [ ] Learning
- [ ] Endurance training
- [ ] Gathering loved ones
- [ ] Seeing new things!
- [ ] ----------------------------------
- [ ] ----------------------------------
- [ ] ----------------------------------

IMMERSIVE EXPERIENCES

- [ ] Cultural/historical
- [ ] Volunteering
- [ ] Park programs
- [ ] Junior Ranger program
- [ ] NPS-guided night walks
- [ ] School/youth trips
- [ ] Teacher/educator programs
- [ ] Professional development
- [ ] ----------------------------------
- [ ] ----------------------------------
- [ ] ----------------------------------

ADVENTURE GOALS

- [ ] Hiking big trails
- [ ] Easy day hikes
- [ ] Cycling/mountain biking/fat biking
- [ ] Kayaking/canoeing/SUP
- [ ] Trail running
- [ ] Rafting
- [ ] Swimming
- [ ] Backpacking
- [ ] Wildlife viewing
- [ ] Scenic drives
- [ ] Fishing/angling
- [ ] Mountaineering
- [ ] Climbing/bouldering
- [ ] Photography
- [ ] Birdwatching
- [ ] Stargazing
- [ ] Cultural immersion
- [ ] Endurance training
- [ ] Picnicking
- [ ] ----------------------------------

PHOTOGRAPHY PLANS

- [ ] Wildlife
- [ ] Birds
- [ ] Landscapes
- [ ] Night skies
- [ ] People
- [ ] Cultural artifacts
- [ ] Macro/abstract
- [ ] Family pictures
- [ ] Selfies
- [ ] ----------------------------------

ADDITIONAL NOTES

PACK FOR YOUR TRIP!

Park name: ....

HEALTH & PERSONAL ITEMS

- [ ] Premade first aid kit
- [ ] Wildlife/insect protection
- [ ] Medications
- [ ] ....
- [ ] ....
- [ ] Supplements
- [ ] ....
- [ ] ....
- [ ] Eyeglasses/contacts
- [ ] Sun/wind/snow protection (eyes/skin/face)
- [ ] Facial tissues
- [ ] Bug spray
- [ ] Antibacterial wipes
- [ ] ....
- [ ] ....

ELECTRONICS

- [ ] Camera
  - [ ] Tripod
  - [ ] Lenses/lens cloths
  - [ ] Memory cards
  - [ ] Batteries & charger
- [ ] Weather protection
- [ ] External charging device
- [ ] Phone & charging cord
- [ ] Mobile Wi-Fi device
- [ ] Electronic tablet
- [ ] Satellite phone
- [ ] Personal locater beacon
- [ ] ....

CLOTHING/SHOES

- [ ] Insulated jacket
- [ ] Rain jacket/pants
- [ ] Thermal layers
- [ ] Wicked/quick-dry clothing
- [ ] Loose-fitting shirts
- [ ] Loose-fitting pants
- [ ] Hiking pants/shorts
- [ ] Short-sleeved/sleeveless shirts
- [ ] Full winter gear
- [ ] ....
- [ ] ....
- [ ] ....
- [ ] Leisurewear
- [ ] Beachwear
- [ ] Hiking shoes
- [ ] Athletic shoes
- [ ] Water shoes
- [ ] Sandals/flip-flops
- [ ] Neck gaiter
- [ ] Sun hat/cap
- [ ] Stocking cap
- [ ] Socks + extra pair
- [ ] Undergarments
- [ ] Gloves/mittens
- [ ] ....
- [ ] ....
- [ ] ....
- [ ] ....
- [ ] ....
- [ ] ....

OUTDOOR GEAR

- [ ] Hiking poles
- [ ] Tent
- [ ] Sleeping bag
- [ ] Sleeping pad
- [ ] Pillow
- [ ] Shade tent
- [ ] Emergency space blanket
- [ ] Tarp
- [ ] Daypack
- [ ] Headlamp(s)
- [ ] Lantern(s)
- [ ] Water filter & iodine tablets
- [ ] Large refillable water jug
- [ ] Portable stove
- [ ] Hot beverage thermos
- [ ] Nylon hammock
- [ ] Throw blanket
- [ ] Reusable dishes/cutlery
- [ ] Hand warmers
- [ ] ....
- [ ] ....
- [ ] ....
- [ ] ....
- [ ] ....
- [ ] ....
- [ ] ....
- [ ] ....
- [ ] ....

FOOD & DRINK

- [ ] Water
- [ ] Refillable water bottle
- [ ] Energy drinks with electrolytes
- [ ] Protein-packed snacks
- [ ] Salty, easy-to-digest snacks
- [ ] Dehydrated food
- [ ] No-cook food items
- [ ] ....
- [ ] ....
- [ ] ....
- [ ] ....
- [ ] ....
- [ ] ....
- [ ] ....
- [ ] ....
- [ ] ....
- [ ] ....
- [ ] ....
- [ ] ....
- [ ] ....
- [ ] ....
- [ ] ....
- [ ] ....

PARK-SPECIFIC

- [ ] *The National Parks Journal*!
- [ ] Permits
- [ ] Guidebooks
- [ ] Park map
- [ ] ....
- [ ] ....
- [ ] ....
- [ ] ....
- [ ] ....
- [ ] ....

MISCELLANEOUS

- [ ] Duct tape
- [ ] Multipurpose tool
- [ ] Knife
- [ ] Scissors
- [ ] Can opener
- [ ] Matches/lighter/ firestarter
- [ ] Hatchet
- [ ] Whistle
- [ ] Bandana
- [ ] Quick-dry towels
- [ ] Waterproof bags
- [ ] Ziplock bags
- [ ] Trash bags
- [ ] Paper towels
- [ ] Bear can
- [ ] Binoculars
- [ ] Deck of cards/games
- [ ] Driver's license, registration, insurance, etc.
- [ ] Spare tire/jack
- [ ] Wiper blades
- [ ] Small amount of cash
- [ ] ....
- [ ] ....
- [ ] ....
- [ ] ....
- [ ] ....
- [ ] ....
- [ ] ....
- [ ] ....
- [ ] ....
- [ ] ....
- [ ] ....
- [ ] ....
- [ ] ....
- [ ] ....
- [ ] ....

PERSONALIZED LIST

- [ ] ....
- [ ] ....
- [ ] ....
- [ ] ....
- [ ] ....
- [ ] ....
- [ ] ....
- [ ] ....
- [ ] ....
- [ ] ....

TO BUY

- [ ] ....
- [ ] ....
- [ ] ....
- [ ] ....
- [ ] ....
- [ ] ....
- [ ] ....
- [ ] ....
- [ ] ....
- [ ] ....

ADDITIONAL NOTES

....
....
....
....
....
....
....
....
....
....
....
....

RECORD YOUR TRIP!

Park name: ....

State/territory: ....

Dates visited: ....

Nearby sites visited: ....

ARROWHEAD RATING!

⬥ 5 — Epic & life-changing experience
⬥ 4 — Want to learn everything about this park!
⬥ 3 — See why this place is so special
⬥ 2 — Happy I went and had some good times
⬥ 1 — Once and done!

FAVORITE CAMPSITE OR LODGING: ....

....

PEAK EXPERIENCE: ....

....

FAVORITE ADVENTURE: ....

....

FAVORITE LOCATION: ....

....

FAVORITE PHOTO: ....

....

BEST WILDLIFE SIGHTING: ....

....

FUN THING(S) I LEARNED ABOUT THE PARK: ....

....

INTERESTING PEOPLE MET ALONG MY JOURNEY: --

VALUABLE RESOURCE(S) DISCOVERED ALONG THE WAY: --

FOOD I COULDN'T LIVE WITHOUT: ---

THE BIGGEST CHALLENGE I FACED: --

I WAS MOST PREPARED WHEN: ---

WISH I KNEW BEFORE I WENT: --

WISH I WOULD HAVE BROUGHT: --

MOST USEFUL PIECE OF GEAR: --

MOST VALUABLE TOOL: ---

MOST USEFUL PIECE OF ADVICE: --

TIPS FOR OTHER TRAVELERS: ---

ADDITIONAL NOTES: ---

PLAN YOUR TRIP!

Park name: ....

State/territory: .... Temperature range: ....

Planned dates: .... Altitude range: ....

Time zone: .... Latitude/longitude: ....

COMMITMENT LEVEL

- 6 — Full throttle, all-in adventure time!
- 5 — Bring on a big challenge!
- 4 — Many trails, sites, & adventures planned!
- 3 — Rolling where the wind blows me!
- 2 — Tons to do without breaking a big sweat!
- 1 — Easy-going, leisurely days...

SEASON OF VISIT
- [ ] Spring
- [ ] Summer
- [ ] Autumn
- [ ] Winter

TOURING/SUPPORT
- [ ] Self-guided
- [ ] Privately guided
- [ ] Chartered trip
- [ ] Group trip
- [ ] Volunteering
- [ ] Ranger-led tours
- [ ] Instructional classes
- [ ] Special events
- [ ] ....
- [ ] ....
- [ ] ....
- [ ] ....
- [ ] ....

PARK TRANSPORT
- [ ] Car
- [ ] Bus
- [ ] RV/travel trailer
- [ ] Boat
- [ ] Float plane/bush plane
- [ ] Helicopter
- [ ] Tour bus
- [ ] All-terrain vehicle
- [ ] ....

PARK ITEMS TO PICK UP
- [ ] NPS annual pass
- [ ] NPS parks passport
- [ ] Pins, patches, & stickers
- [ ] Hiking stick medallions
- [ ] NPS maps & literature
- [ ] ....
- [ ] ....
- [ ] ....

RESOURCES/CONTACTS
- [ ] NPS visitor center(s):
  ....
- [ ] Wilderness permit(s):
  ....
- [ ] Tour company:
  ....
- [ ] Local guide(s):
  ....
- [ ] Local gear outfitter(s):
  ....
- [ ] Emergency services:
  ....
- [ ] Miscellaneous contact:
  ....
- [ ] Miscellaneous contact:
  ....

MAIN ACCOMMODATIONS
- [ ] NPS lodge
- [ ] Hotel
- [ ] RV/travel trailer
- [ ] Tent camping
- [ ] Backcountry camping
- [ ] Staying with friends
- [ ] Houseboat
- [ ] Cruise ship
- [ ] Van/car
- [ ] ....

AMENITIES

- [ ] Campgrounds
  - [ ] Standard
  - [ ] RV
  - [ ] Primitive
  - [ ] Day use only
  - [ ] Group
- [ ] Plumbed bathrooms
- [ ] Showers
- [ ] Park store
- [ ] Wi-Fi
- [ ] NPS amphitheater
- [ ] Pet-friendly
- [ ] --------------------------------
- [ ] --------------------------------

IN-TOW

- [ ] Spouse/partner
- [ ] Children
- [ ] Pets
- [ ] Friends
- [ ] Extended family
- [ ] Boatloads of gear!
- [ ] --------------------------------
- [ ] --------------------------------

ADVANCED PLANNING

- [ ] Physical training?

- [ ] Seasonal aspects?

- [ ] Obtained permits?

- [ ] Purchased gear?

FINAL SAFETY CHECKS

- [ ] Left your trip plan with an emergency contact back home?
- [ ] Reviewed basic emergency aid procedures?
- [ ] Additional forms/permits needed?
- [ ] Checked on closures/mandates that might affect your travel?
- [ ] --------------------------------
- [ ] --------------------------------
- [ ] --------------------------------

MAIN GOALS

- [ ] Solitude
- [ ] Active adventure
- [ ] Creative pursuits
- [ ] Learning
- [ ] Endurance training
- [ ] Gathering loved ones
- [ ] Seeing new things!
- [ ] --------------------------------
- [ ] --------------------------------
- [ ] --------------------------------

IMMERSIVE EXPERIENCES

- [ ] Cultural/historical
- [ ] Volunteering
- [ ] Park programs
- [ ] Junior Ranger program
- [ ] NPS-guided night walks
- [ ] School/youth trips
- [ ] Teacher/educator programs
- [ ] Professional development
- [ ] --------------------------------
- [ ] --------------------------------
- [ ] --------------------------------

ADVENTURE GOALS

- [ ] Hiking big trails
- [ ] Easy day hikes
- [ ] Cycling/mountain biking/fat biking
- [ ] Kayaking/canoeing/SUP
- [ ] Trail running
- [ ] Rafting
- [ ] Swimming
- [ ] Backpacking
- [ ] Wildlife viewing
- [ ] Scenic drives
- [ ] Fishing/angling
- [ ] Mountaineering
- [ ] Climbing/bouldering
- [ ] Photography
- [ ] Birdwatching
- [ ] Stargazing
- [ ] Cultural immersion
- [ ] Endurance training
- [ ] Picnicking
- [ ] --------------------------------

PHOTOGRAPHY PLANS

- [ ] Wildlife
- [ ] Birds
- [ ] Landscapes
- [ ] Night skies
- [ ] People
- [ ] Cultural artifacts
- [ ] Macro/abstract
- [ ] Family pictures
- [ ] Selfies
- [ ] --------------------------------

ADDITIONAL NOTES

PACK FOR YOUR TRIP!

Park name: ....

HEALTH & PERSONAL ITEMS

- [ ] Premade first aid kit
- [ ] Wildlife/insect protection
- [ ] Medications
- [ ] ....
- [ ] ....
- [ ] Supplements
- [ ] ....
- [ ] ....
- [ ] Eyeglasses/contacts
- [ ] Sun/wind/snow protection (eyes/skin/face)
- [ ] Facial tissues
- [ ] Bug spray
- [ ] Antibacterial wipes
- [ ] ....
- [ ] ....

ELECTRONICS

- [ ] Camera
  - [ ] Tripod
  - [ ] Lenses/lens cloths
  - [ ] Memory cards
  - [ ] Batteries & charger
- [ ] Weather protection
- [ ] External charging device
- [ ] Phone & charging cord
- [ ] Mobile Wi-Fi device
- [ ] Electronic tablet
- [ ] Satellite phone
- [ ] Personal locater beacon
- [ ] ....

CLOTHING/SHOES

- [ ] Insulated jacket
- [ ] Rain jacket/pants
- [ ] Thermal layers
- [ ] Wicked/quick-dry clothing
- [ ] Loose-fitting shirts
- [ ] Loose-fitting pants
- [ ] Hiking pants/shorts
- [ ] Short-sleeved/sleeveless shirts
- [ ] Full winter gear
- [ ] ....
- [ ] ....
- [ ] ....
- [ ] Leisurewear
- [ ] Beachwear
- [ ] Hiking shoes
- [ ] Athletic shoes
- [ ] Water shoes
- [ ] Sandals/flip-flops
- [ ] Neck gaiter
- [ ] Sun hat/cap
- [ ] Stocking cap
- [ ] Socks + extra pair
- [ ] Undergarments
- [ ] Gloves/mittens
- [ ] ....
- [ ] ....
- [ ] ....
- [ ] ....
- [ ] ....
- [ ] ....
- [ ] ....

OUTDOOR GEAR

- [ ] Hiking poles
- [ ] Tent
- [ ] Sleeping bag
- [ ] Sleeping pad
- [ ] Pillow
- [ ] Shade tent
- [ ] Emergency space blanket
- [ ] Tarp
- [ ] Daypack
- [ ] Headlamp(s)
- [ ] Lantern(s)
- [ ] Water filter & iodine tablets
- [ ] Large refillable water jug
- [ ] Portable stove
- [ ] Hot beverage thermos
- [ ] Nylon hammock
- [ ] Throw blanket
- [ ] Reusable dishes/cutlery
- [ ] Hand warmers
- [ ] ....
- [ ] ....
- [ ] ....
- [ ] ....
- [ ] ....
- [ ] ....
- [ ] ....
- [ ] ....
- [ ] ....
- [ ] ....

FOOD & DRINK

- [ ] Water
- [ ] Refillable water bottle
- [ ] Energy drinks with electrolytes
- [ ] Protein-packed snacks
- [ ] Salty, easy-to-digest snacks
- [ ] Dehydrated food
- [ ] No-cook food items
- [ ] ....
- [ ] ....
- [ ] ....
- [ ] ....
- [ ] ....
- [ ] ....
- [ ] ....
- [ ] ....
- [ ] ....
- [ ] ....
- [ ] ....
- [ ] ....
- [ ] ....
- [ ] ....
- [ ] ....

PARK-SPECIFIC

- [ ] *The National Parks Journal*!
- [ ] Permits
- [ ] Guidebooks
- [ ] Park map
- [ ] ....
- [ ] ....
- [ ] ....
- [ ] ....
- [ ] ....
- [ ] ....

MISCELLANEOUS

- [ ] Duct tape
- [ ] Multipurpose tool
- [ ] Knife
- [ ] Scissors
- [ ] Can opener
- [ ] Matches/lighter/firestarter
- [ ] Hatchet
- [ ] Whistle
- [ ] Bandana
- [ ] Quick-dry towels
- [ ] Waterproof bags
- [ ] Ziplock bags
- [ ] Trash bags
- [ ] Paper towels
- [ ] Bear can
- [ ] Binoculars
- [ ] Deck of cards/games
- [ ] Driver's license, registration, insurance, etc.
- [ ] Spare tire/jack
- [ ] Wiper blades
- [ ] Small amount of cash
- [ ] ....
- [ ] ....
- [ ] ....
- [ ] ....
- [ ] ....
- [ ] ....
- [ ] ....
- [ ] ....
- [ ] ....
- [ ] ....
- [ ] ....
- [ ] ....
- [ ] ....
- [ ] ....

PERSONALIZED LIST

- [ ] ....
- [ ] ....
- [ ] ....
- [ ] ....
- [ ] ....
- [ ] ....
- [ ] ....
- [ ] ....
- [ ] ....
- [ ] ....

TO BUY

- [ ] ....
- [ ] ....
- [ ] ....
- [ ] ....
- [ ] ....
- [ ] ....
- [ ] ....
- [ ] ....
- [ ] ....

ADDITIONAL NOTES

RECORD YOUR TRIP!

Park name: ....

State/territory: ....

Dates visited: ....

Nearby sites visited: ....

5 — Epic & life-changing experience
4 — Want to learn everything about this park!
3 — See why this place is so special
2 — Happy I went and had some good times
1 — Once and done!

FAVORITE CAMPSITE OR LODGING: ....
....

PEAK EXPERIENCE: ....
....

FAVORITE ADVENTURE: ....
....

FAVORITE LOCATION: ....
....

FAVORITE PHOTO: ....
....

BEST WILDLIFE SIGHTING: ....
....

FUN THING(S) I LEARNED ABOUT THE PARK: ....
....

INTERESTING PEOPLE MET ALONG MY JOURNEY: --

VALUABLE RESOURCE(S) DISCOVERED ALONG THE WAY: --

FOOD I COULDN'T LIVE WITHOUT: ---

THE BIGGEST CHALLENGE I FACED: --

I WAS MOST PREPARED WHEN: ---

WISH I KNEW BEFORE I WENT: --

WISH I WOULD HAVE BROUGHT: --

MOST USEFUL PIECE OF GEAR: --

MOST VALUABLE TOOL: --

MOST USEFUL PIECE OF ADVICE: --

TIPS FOR OTHER TRAVELERS: ---

ADDITIONAL NOTES: --

PLAN YOUR TRIP!

Park name: ....

State/territory: .... Temperature range: ....

Planned dates: .... Altitude range: ....

Time zone: .... Latitude/longitude: ....

COMMITMENT LEVEL

6 — Full throttle, all-in adventure time!

5 — Bring on a big challenge!

4 — Many trails, sites, & adventures planned!

3 — Rolling where the wind blows me!

2 — Tons to do without breaking a big sweat!

1 — Easy-going, leisurely days...

SEASON OF VISIT

☐ Spring
☐ Summer
☐ Autumn
☐ Winter

TOURING/SUPPORT

☐ Self-guided
☐ Privately guided
☐ Chartered trip
☐ Group trip
☐ Volunteering
☐ Ranger-led tours
☐ Instructional classes
☐ Special events
....
....
....
....

PARK TRANSPORT

☐ Car
☐ Bus
☐ RV/travel trailer
☐ Boat
☐ Float plane/bush plane
☐ Helicopter
☐ Tour bus
☐ All-terrain vehicle
☐ ....

PARK ITEMS TO PICK UP

☐ NPS annual pass
☐ NPS parks passport
☐ Pins, patches, & stickers
☐ Hiking stick medallions
☐ NPS maps & literature
☐
☐
☐

RESOURCES/CONTACTS

☐ NPS visitor center(s):
....
☐ Wilderness permit(s):
....
☐ Tour company:
....
☐ Local guide(s):
....
☐ Local gear outfitter(s):
....
☐ Emergency services:
....
☐ Miscellaneous contact:
....
☐ Miscellaneous contact:
....

MAIN ACCOMMODATIONS

☐ NPS lodge
☐ Hotel
☐ RV/travel trailer
☐ Tent camping
☐ Backcountry camping
☐ Staying with friends
☐ Houseboat
☐ Cruise ship
☐ Van/car
☐ ....
☐ ....

AMENITIES

- [ ] Campgrounds
  - [ ] Standard
  - [ ] RV
  - [ ] Primitive
  - [ ] Day use only
  - [ ] Group
- [ ] Plumbed bathrooms
- [ ] Showers
- [ ] Park store
- [ ] Wi-Fi
- [ ] NPS amphitheater
- [ ] Pet-friendly
- [ ] --
- [ ] --

IN-TOW

- [ ] Spouse/partner
- [ ] Children
- [ ] Pets
- [ ] Friends
- [ ] Extended family
- [ ] Boatloads of gear!
- [ ] --
- [ ] --

ADVANCED PLANNING

- [ ] Physical training?

- [ ] Seasonal aspects?

- [ ] Obtained permits?

- [ ] Purchased gear?

FINAL SAFETY CHECKS

- [ ] Left your trip plan with an emergency contact back home?
- [ ] Reviewed basic emergency aid procedures?
- [ ] Additional forms/permits needed?
- [ ] Checked on closures/mandates that might affect your travel?
- [ ] --
- [ ] --
- [ ] --

MAIN GOALS

- [ ] Solitude
- [ ] Active adventure
- [ ] Creative pursuits
- [ ] Learning
- [ ] Endurance training
- [ ] Gathering loved ones
- [ ] Seeing new things!
- [ ] --
- [ ] --
- [ ] --

IMMERSIVE EXPERIENCES

- [ ] Cultural/historical
- [ ] Volunteering
- [ ] Park programs
- [ ] Junior Ranger program
- [ ] NPS-guided night walks
- [ ] School/youth trips
- [ ] Teacher/educator programs
- [ ] Professional development
- [ ] --
- [ ] --
- [ ] --

ADVENTURE GOALS

- [ ] Hiking big trails
- [ ] Easy day hikes
- [ ] Cycling/mountain biking/fat biking
- [ ] Kayaking/canoeing/SUP
- [ ] Trail running
- [ ] Rafting
- [ ] Swimming
- [ ] Backpacking
- [ ] Wildlife viewing
- [ ] Scenic drives
- [ ] Fishing/angling
- [ ] Mountaineering
- [ ] Climbing/bouldering
- [ ] Photography
- [ ] Birdwatching
- [ ] Stargazing
- [ ] Cultural immersion
- [ ] Endurance training
- [ ] Picnicking
- [ ] --

PHOTOGRAPHY PLANS

- [ ] Wildlife
- [ ] Birds
- [ ] Landscapes
- [ ] Night skies
- [ ] People
- [ ] Cultural artifacts
- [ ] Macro/abstract
- [ ] Family pictures
- [ ] Selfies
- [ ] --

ADDITIONAL NOTES

PACK FOR YOUR TRIP!

Park name: ....

HEALTH & PERSONAL ITEMS

- [ ] Premade first aid kit
- [ ] Wildlife/insect protection
- [ ] Medications
- [ ] ....
- [ ] Supplements
- [ ] ....
- [ ] Eyeglasses/contacts
- [ ] Sun/wind/snow protection (eyes/skin/face)
- [ ] Facial tissues
- [ ] Bug spray
- [ ] Antibacterial wipes
- [ ] ....
- [ ] ....

ELECTRONICS

- [ ] Camera
  - [ ] Tripod
  - [ ] Lenses/lens cloths
  - [ ] Memory cards
  - [ ] Batteries & charger
- [ ] Weather protection
- [ ] External charging device
- [ ] Phone & charging cord
- [ ] Mobile Wi-Fi device
- [ ] Electronic tablet
- [ ] Satellite phone
- [ ] Personal locater beacon
- [ ] ....

CLOTHING/SHOES

- [ ] Insulated jacket
- [ ] Rain jacket/pants
- [ ] Thermal layers
- [ ] Wicked/quick-dry clothing
- [ ] Loose-fitting shirts
- [ ] Loose-fitting pants
- [ ] Hiking pants/shorts
- [ ] Short-sleeved/sleeveless shirts
- [ ] Full winter gear
- [ ] ....
- [ ] ....
- [ ] ....
- [ ] Leisurewear
- [ ] Beachwear
- [ ] Hiking shoes
- [ ] Athletic shoes
- [ ] Water shoes
- [ ] Sandals/flip-flops
- [ ] Neck gaiter
- [ ] Sun hat/cap
- [ ] Stocking cap
- [ ] Socks + extra pair
- [ ] Undergarments
- [ ] Gloves/mittens
- [ ] ....
- [ ] ....
- [ ] ....
- [ ] ....
- [ ] ....
- [ ] ....

OUTDOOR GEAR

- [ ] Hiking poles
- [ ] Tent
- [ ] Sleeping bag
- [ ] Sleeping pad
- [ ] Pillow
- [ ] Shade tent
- [ ] Emergency space blanket
- [ ] Tarp
- [ ] Daypack
- [ ] Headlamp(s)
- [ ] Lantern(s)
- [ ] Water filter & iodine tablets
- [ ] Large refillable water jug
- [ ] Portable stove
- [ ] Hot beverage thermos
- [ ] Nylon hammock
- [ ] Throw blanket
- [ ] Reusable dishes/cutlery
- [ ] Hand warmers
- [ ] ....
- [ ] ....
- [ ] ....
- [ ] ....
- [ ] ....
- [ ] ....
- [ ] ....
- [ ] ....
- [ ] ....
- [ ] ....

FOOD & DRINK

- [ ] Water
- [ ] Refillable water bottle
- [ ] Energy drinks with electrolytes
- [ ] Protein-packed snacks
- [ ] Salty, easy-to-digest snacks
- [ ] Dehydrated food
- [ ] No-cook food items
- [ ] ---------------------------------
- [ ] ---------------------------------
- [ ] ---------------------------------
- [ ] ---------------------------------
- [ ] ---------------------------------
- [ ] ---------------------------------
- [ ] ---------------------------------
- [ ] ---------------------------------
- [ ] ---------------------------------
- [ ] ---------------------------------
- [ ] ---------------------------------
- [ ] ---------------------------------
- [ ] ---------------------------------
- [ ] ---------------------------------
- [ ] ---------------------------------

PARK-SPECIFIC

- [ ] *The National Parks Journal*!
- [ ] Permits
- [ ] Guidebooks
- [ ] Park map
- [ ] ---------------------------------
- [ ] ---------------------------------
- [ ] ---------------------------------
- [ ] ---------------------------------
- [ ] ---------------------------------
- [ ] ---------------------------------

MISCELLANEOUS

- [ ] Duct tape
- [ ] Multipurpose tool
- [ ] Knife
- [ ] Scissors
- [ ] Can opener
- [ ] Matches/lighter/firestarter
- [ ] Hatchet
- [ ] Whistle
- [ ] Bandana
- [ ] Quick-dry towels
- [ ] Waterproof bags
- [ ] Ziplock bags
- [ ] Trash bags
- [ ] Paper towels
- [ ] Bear can
- [ ] Binoculars
- [ ] Deck of cards/games
- [ ] Driver's license, registration, insurance, etc.
- [ ] Spare tire/jack
- [ ] Wiper blades
- [ ] Small amount of cash
- [ ] ---------------------------------
- [ ] ---------------------------------
- [ ] ---------------------------------
- [ ] ---------------------------------
- [ ] ---------------------------------
- [ ] ---------------------------------
- [ ] ---------------------------------
- [ ] ---------------------------------
- [ ] ---------------------------------
- [ ] ---------------------------------
- [ ] ---------------------------------
- [ ] ---------------------------------
- [ ] ---------------------------------

PERSONALIZED LIST

- [ ] ---------------------------------
- [ ] ---------------------------------
- [ ] ---------------------------------
- [ ] ---------------------------------
- [ ] ---------------------------------
- [ ] ---------------------------------
- [ ] ---------------------------------
- [ ] ---------------------------------
- [ ] ---------------------------------
- [ ] ---------------------------------
- [ ] ---------------------------------

TO BUY

- [ ] ---------------------------------
- [ ] ---------------------------------
- [ ] ---------------------------------
- [ ] ---------------------------------
- [ ] ---------------------------------
- [ ] ---------------------------------
- [ ] ---------------------------------
- [ ] ---------------------------------
- [ ] ---------------------------------
- [ ] ---------------------------------

ADDITIONAL NOTES

RECORD YOUR TRIP!

Park name: ....

State/territory: ....

Dates visited: ....

Nearby sites visited: ....

ARROWHEAD RATING!

- 5 — Epic & life-changing experience
- 4 — Want to learn everything about this park!
- 3 — See why this place is so special
- 2 — Happy I went and had some good times
- 1 — Once and done!

FAVORITE CAMPSITE OR LODGING: ....

....

PEAK EXPERIENCE: ....

....

FAVORITE ADVENTURE: ....

....

FAVORITE LOCATION: ....

....

FAVORITE PHOTO: ....

....

BEST WILDLIFE SIGHTING: ....

....

FUN THING(S) I LEARNED ABOUT THE PARK: ....

....

INTERESTING PEOPLE MET ALONG MY JOURNEY:

VALUABLE RESOURCE(S) DISCOVERED ALONG THE WAY:

FOOD I COULDN'T LIVE WITHOUT:

THE BIGGEST CHALLENGE I FACED:

I WAS MOST PREPARED WHEN:

WISH I KNEW BEFORE I WENT:

WISH I WOULD HAVE BROUGHT:

MOST USEFUL PIECE OF GEAR:

MOST VALUABLE TOOL:

MOST USEFUL PIECE OF ADVICE:

TIPS FOR OTHER TRAVELERS:

ADDITIONAL NOTES:

PLAN YOUR TRIP!

Park name: ....

State/territory: ....   Temperature range: ....

Planned dates: ....   Altitude range: ....

Time zone: ....   Latitude/longitude: ....

COMMITMENT LEVEL

6 — Full throttle, all-in adventure time!

5 — Bring on a big challenge!

4 — Many trails, sites, & adventures planned!

3 — Rolling where the wind blows me!

2 — Tons to do without breaking a big sweat!

1 — Easy-going, leisurely days...

SEASON OF VISIT

- [ ] Spring
- [ ] Summer
- [ ] Autumn
- [ ] Winter

TOURING/SUPPORT

- [ ] Self-guided
- [ ] Privately guided
- [ ] Chartered trip
- [ ] Group trip
- [ ] Volunteering
- [ ] Ranger-led tours
- [ ] Instructional classes
- [ ] Special events
- [ ] ....
- [ ] ....
- [ ] ....
- [ ] ....
- [ ] ....

PARK TRANSPORT

- [ ] Car
- [ ] Bus
- [ ] RV/travel trailer
- [ ] Boat
- [ ] Float plane/bush plane
- [ ] Helicopter
- [ ] Tour bus
- [ ] All-terrain vehicle
- [ ] ....

PARK ITEMS TO PICK UP

- [ ] NPS annual pass
- [ ] NPS parks passport
- [ ] Pins, patches, & stickers
- [ ] Hiking stick medallions
- [ ] NPS maps & literature
- [ ] ....
- [ ] ....
- [ ] ....

RESOURCES/CONTACTS

- [ ] NPS visitor center(s):
- [ ] Wilderness permit(s):
- [ ] Tour company:
- [ ] Local guide(s):
- [ ] Local gear outfitter(s):
- [ ] Emergency services:
- [ ] Miscellaneous contact:
- [ ] Miscellaneous contact:

MAIN ACCOMMODATIONS

- [ ] NPS lodge
- [ ] Hotel
- [ ] RV/travel trailer
- [ ] Tent camping
- [ ] Backcountry camping
- [ ] Staying with friends
- [ ] Houseboat
- [ ] Cruise ship
- [ ] Van/car
- [ ] ....
- [ ] ....

AMENITIES

- [ ] Campgrounds
  - [ ] Standard
  - [ ] RV
  - [ ] Primitive
  - [ ] Day use only
  - [ ] Group
- [ ] Plumbed bathrooms
- [ ] Showers
- [ ] Park store
- [ ] Wi-Fi
- [ ] NPS amphitheater
- [ ] Pet-friendly
- [ ] ----------------------------------
- [ ] ----------------------------------

IN-TOW

- [ ] Spouse/partner
- [ ] Children
- [ ] Pets
- [ ] Friends
- [ ] Extended family
- [ ] Boatloads of gear!
- [ ] ----------------------------------
- [ ] ----------------------------------

ADVANCED PLANNING

- [ ] Physical training?

- [ ] Seasonal aspects?

- [ ] Obtained permits?

- [ ] Purchased gear?

FINAL SAFETY CHECKS

- [ ] Left your trip plan with an emergency contact back home?
- [ ] Reviewed basic emergency aid procedures?
- [ ] Additional forms/permits needed?
- [ ] Checked on closures/mandates that might affect your travel?
- [ ] ----------------------------------
- [ ] ----------------------------------
- [ ] ----------------------------------

MAIN GOALS

- [ ] Solitude
- [ ] Active adventure
- [ ] Creative pursuits
- [ ] Learning
- [ ] Endurance training
- [ ] Gathering loved ones
- [ ] Seeing new things!
- [ ] ----------------------------------
- [ ] ----------------------------------
- [ ] ----------------------------------

IMMERSIVE EXPERIENCES

- [ ] Cultural/historical
- [ ] Volunteering
- [ ] Park programs
- [ ] Junior Ranger program
- [ ] NPS-guided night walks
- [ ] School/youth trips
- [ ] Teacher/educator programs
- [ ] Professional development
- [ ] ----------------------------------
- [ ] ----------------------------------
- [ ] ----------------------------------

ADVENTURE GOALS

- [ ] Hiking big trails
- [ ] Easy day hikes
- [ ] Cycling/mountain biking/fat biking
- [ ] Kayaking/canoeing/SUP
- [ ] Trail running
- [ ] Rafting
- [ ] Swimming
- [ ] Backpacking
- [ ] Wildlife viewing
- [ ] Scenic drives
- [ ] Fishing/angling
- [ ] Mountaineering
- [ ] Climbing/bouldering
- [ ] Photography
- [ ] Birdwatching
- [ ] Stargazing
- [ ] Cultural immersion
- [ ] Endurance training
- [ ] Picnicking
- [ ] ----------------------------------

PHOTOGRAPHY PLANS

- [ ] Wildlife
- [ ] Birds
- [ ] Landscapes
- [ ] Night skies
- [ ] People
- [ ] Cultural artifacts
- [ ] Macro/abstract
- [ ] Family pictures
- [ ] Selfies
- [ ] ----------------------------------

ADDITIONAL NOTES

PACK FOR YOUR TRIP!

Park name: ....

HEALTH & PERSONAL ITEMS
- [ ] Premade first aid kit
- [ ] Wildlife/insect protection
- [ ] Medications
- [ ] ....
- [ ] ....
- [ ] Supplements
- [ ] ....
- [ ] ....
- [ ] Eyeglasses/contacts
- [ ] Sun/wind/snow protection (eyes/skin/face)
- [ ] Facial tissues
- [ ] Bug spray
- [ ] Antibacterial wipes
- [ ] ....
- [ ] ....

ELECTRONICS
- [ ] Camera
  - [ ] Tripod
  - [ ] Lenses/lens cloths
  - [ ] Memory cards
  - [ ] Batteries & charger
- [ ] Weather protection
- [ ] External charging device
- [ ] Phone & charging cord
- [ ] Mobile Wi-Fi device
- [ ] Electronic tablet
- [ ] Satellite phone
- [ ] Personal locater beacon
- [ ] ....

CLOTHING/SHOES
- [ ] Insulated jacket
- [ ] Rain jacket/pants
- [ ] Thermal layers
- [ ] Wicked/quick-dry clothing
- [ ] Loose-fitting shirts
- [ ] Loose-fitting pants
- [ ] Hiking pants/shorts
- [ ] Short-sleeved/sleeveless shirts
- [ ] Full winter gear
- [ ] ....
- [ ] ....
- [ ] ....
- [ ] Leisurewear
- [ ] Beachwear
- [ ] Hiking shoes
- [ ] Athletic shoes
- [ ] Water shoes
- [ ] Sandals/flip-flops
- [ ] Neck gaiter
- [ ] Sun hat/cap
- [ ] Stocking cap
- [ ] Socks + extra pair
- [ ] Undergarments
- [ ] Gloves/mittens
- [ ] ....
- [ ] ....
- [ ] ....
- [ ] ....
- [ ] ....
- [ ] ....
- [ ] ....

OUTDOOR GEAR
- [ ] Hiking poles
- [ ] Tent
- [ ] Sleeping bag
- [ ] Sleeping pad
- [ ] Pillow
- [ ] Shade tent
- [ ] Emergency space blanket
- [ ] Tarp
- [ ] Daypack
- [ ] Headlamp(s)
- [ ] Lantern(s)
- [ ] Water filter & iodine tablets
- [ ] Large refillable water jug
- [ ] Portable stove
- [ ] Hot beverage thermos
- [ ] Nylon hammock
- [ ] Throw blanket
- [ ] Reusable dishes/cutlery
- [ ] Hand warmers
- [ ] ....
- [ ] ....
- [ ] ....
- [ ] ....
- [ ] ....
- [ ] ....
- [ ] ....
- [ ] ....
- [ ] ....
- [ ] ....

FOOD & DRINK

- [ ] Water
- [ ] Refillable water bottle
- [ ] Energy drinks with electrolytes
- [ ] Protein-packed snacks
- [ ] Salty, easy-to-digest snacks
- [ ] Dehydrated food
- [ ] No-cook food items
- [ ] ....
- [ ] ....
- [ ] ....
- [ ] ....
- [ ] ....
- [ ] ....
- [ ] ....
- [ ] ....
- [ ] ....
- [ ] ....
- [ ] ....
- [ ] ....
- [ ] ....
- [ ] ....

PARK-SPECIFIC

- [ ] *The National Parks Journal*!
- [ ] Permits
- [ ] Guidebooks
- [ ] Park map
- [ ] ....
- [ ] ....
- [ ] ....
- [ ] ....
- [ ] ....
- [ ] ....
- [ ] ....

MISCELLANEOUS

- [ ] Duct tape
- [ ] Multipurpose tool
- [ ] Knife
- [ ] Scissors
- [ ] Can opener
- [ ] Matches/lighter/firestarter
- [ ] Hatchet
- [ ] Whistle
- [ ] Bandana
- [ ] Quick-dry towels
- [ ] Waterproof bags
- [ ] Ziplock bags
- [ ] Trash bags
- [ ] Paper towels
- [ ] Bear can
- [ ] Binoculars
- [ ] Deck of cards/games
- [ ] Driver's license, registration, insurance, etc.
- [ ] Spare tire/jack
- [ ] Wiper blades
- [ ] Small amount of cash
- [ ] ....
- [ ] ....
- [ ] ....
- [ ] ....
- [ ] ....
- [ ] ....
- [ ] ....
- [ ] ....
- [ ] ....
- [ ] ....
- [ ] ....
- [ ] ....
- [ ] ....
- [ ] ....

PERSONALIZED LIST

- [ ] ....
- [ ] ....
- [ ] ....
- [ ] ....
- [ ] ....
- [ ] ....
- [ ] ....
- [ ] ....
- [ ] ....
- [ ] ....

TO BUY

- [ ] ....
- [ ] ....
- [ ] ....
- [ ] ....
- [ ] ....
- [ ] ....
- [ ] ....
- [ ] ....
- [ ] ....

ADDITIONAL NOTES

RECORD YOUR TRIP!

Park name: ....

State/territory: ....

Dates visited: ....

Nearby sites visited: ....

ARROWHEAD RATING!

5 — Epic & life-changing experience

4 — Want to learn everything about this park!

3 — See why this place is so special

2 — Happy I went and had some good times

1 — Once and done!

FAVORITE CAMPSITE OR LODGING: ....

....

PEAK EXPERIENCE: ....

....

FAVORITE ADVENTURE: ....

....

FAVORITE LOCATION: ....

....

FAVORITE PHOTO: ....

....

BEST WILDLIFE SIGHTING: ....

....

FUN THING(S) I LEARNED ABOUT THE PARK: ....

....

INTERESTING PEOPLE MET ALONG MY JOURNEY: ------------------------------

----

VALUABLE RESOURCE(S) DISCOVERED ALONG THE WAY: -------------------

----

FOOD I COULDN'T LIVE WITHOUT: ---------------------------------------

----

THE BIGGEST CHALLENGE I FACED: --------------------------------------

----

I WAS MOST PREPARED WHEN: ---

WISH I KNEW BEFORE I WENT: --

WISH I WOULD HAVE BROUGHT: --

MOST USEFUL PIECE OF GEAR: --

MOST VALUABLE TOOL: ---

MOST USEFUL PIECE OF ADVICE: --

TIPS FOR OTHER TRAVELERS: ---

ADDITIONAL NOTES: ---

PLAN YOUR TRIP!

Park name: ....

State/territory: ....   Temperature range: ....

Planned dates: ....   Altitude range: ....

Time zone: ....   Latitude/longitude: ....

COMMITMENT LEVEL

- 6 — Full throttle, all-in adventure time!
- 5 — Bring on a big challenge!
- 4 — Many trails, sites, & adventures planned!
- 3 — Rolling where the wind blows me!
- 2 — Tons to do without breaking a big sweat!
- 1 — Easy-going, leisurely days...

SEASON OF VISIT

- ☐ Spring
- ☐ Summer
- ☐ Autumn
- ☐ Winter

TOURING/SUPPORT

- ☐ Self-guided
- ☐ Privately guided
- ☐ Chartered trip
- ☐ Group trip
- ☐ Volunteering
- ☐ Ranger-led tours
- ☐ Instructional classes
- ☐ Special events
- ☐ ....
- ☐ ....
- ☐ ....
- ☐ ....
- ☐ ....

PARK TRANSPORT

- ☐ Car
- ☐ Bus
- ☐ RV/travel trailer
- ☐ Boat
- ☐ Float plane/bush plane
- ☐ Helicopter
- ☐ Tour bus
- ☐ All-terrain vehicle
- ☐ ....

PARK ITEMS TO PICK UP

- ☐ NPS annual pass
- ☐ NPS parks passport
- ☐ Pins, patches, & stickers
- ☐ Hiking stick medallions
- ☐ NPS maps & literature
- ☐ ....
- ☐ ....
- ☐ ....

RESOURCES/CONTACTS

- ☐ NPS visitor center(s):
  ....
- ☐ Wilderness permit(s):
  ....
- ☐ Tour company:
  ....
- ☐ Local guide(s):
  ....
- ☐ Local gear outfitter(s):
  ....
- ☐ Emergency services:
  ....
- ☐ Miscellaneous contact:
  ....
- ☐ Miscellaneous contact:
  ....

MAIN ACCOMMODATIONS

- ☐ NPS lodge
- ☐ Hotel
- ☐ RV/travel trailer
- ☐ Tent camping
- ☐ Backcountry camping
- ☐ Staying with friends
- ☐ Houseboat
- ☐ Cruise ship
- ☐ Van/car
- ☐ ....
- ☐ ....

AMENITIES

- [ ] Campgrounds
  - [ ] Standard
  - [ ] RV
  - [ ] Primitive
  - [ ] Day use only
  - [ ] Group
- [ ] Plumbed bathrooms
- [ ] Showers
- [ ] Park store
- [ ] Wi-Fi
- [ ] NPS amphitheater
- [ ] Pet-friendly
- [ ] --------------------------------
- [ ] --------------------------------

IN-TOW

- [ ] Spouse/partner
- [ ] Children
- [ ] Pets
- [ ] Friends
- [ ] Extended family
- [ ] Boatloads of gear!
- [ ] --------------------------------
- [ ] --------------------------------

ADVANCED PLANNING

- [ ] Physical training?

- [ ] Seasonal aspects?

- [ ] Obtained permits?

- [ ] Purchased gear?

FINAL SAFETY CHECKS

- [ ] Left your trip plan with an emergency contact back home?
- [ ] Reviewed basic emergency aid procedures?
- [ ] Additional forms/permits needed?
- [ ] Checked on closures/mandates that might affect your travel?
- [ ] --------------------------------
- [ ] --------------------------------
- [ ] --------------------------------

MAIN GOALS

- [ ] Solitude
- [ ] Active adventure
- [ ] Creative pursuits
- [ ] Learning
- [ ] Endurance training
- [ ] Gathering loved ones
- [ ] Seeing new things!
- [ ] --------------------------------
- [ ] --------------------------------
- [ ] --------------------------------

IMMERSIVE EXPERIENCES

- [ ] Cultural/historical
- [ ] Volunteering
- [ ] Park programs
- [ ] Junior Ranger program
- [ ] NPS-guided night walks
- [ ] School/youth trips
- [ ] Teacher/educator programs
- [ ] Professional development
- [ ] --------------------------------
- [ ] --------------------------------
- [ ] --------------------------------

ADVENTURE GOALS

- [ ] Hiking big trails
- [ ] Easy day hikes
- [ ] Cycling/mountain biking/fat biking
- [ ] Kayaking/canoeing/SUP
- [ ] Trail running
- [ ] Rafting
- [ ] Swimming
- [ ] Backpacking
- [ ] Wildlife viewing
- [ ] Scenic drives
- [ ] Fishing/angling
- [ ] Mountaineering
- [ ] Climbing/bouldering
- [ ] Photography
- [ ] Birdwatching
- [ ] Stargazing
- [ ] Cultural immersion
- [ ] Endurance training
- [ ] Picnicking
- [ ] --------------------------------

PHOTOGRAPHY PLANS

- [ ] Wildlife
- [ ] Birds
- [ ] Landscapes
- [ ] Night skies
- [ ] People
- [ ] Cultural artifacts
- [ ] Macro/abstract
- [ ] Family pictures
- [ ] Selfies
- [ ] --------------------------------

ADDITIONAL NOTES

PACK FOR YOUR TRIP!

Park name: ....

HEALTH & PERSONAL ITEMS

- [ ] Premade first aid kit
- [ ] Wildlife/insect protection
- [ ] Medications
  - ....
  - ....
- [ ] Supplements
  - ....
  - ....
- [ ] Eyeglasses/contacts
- [ ] Sun/wind/snow protection (eyes/skin/face)
- [ ] Facial tissues
- [ ] Bug spray
- [ ] Antibacterial wipes
- [ ] ....
- [ ] ....

ELECTRONICS

- [ ] Camera
  - [ ] Tripod
  - [ ] Lenses/lens cloths
  - [ ] Memory cards
  - [ ] Batteries & charger
- [ ] Weather protection
- [ ] External charging device
- [ ] Phone & charging cord
- [ ] Mobile Wi-Fi device
- [ ] Electronic tablet
- [ ] Satellite phone
- [ ] Personal locater beacon
- [ ] ....

CLOTHING/SHOES

- [ ] Insulated jacket
- [ ] Rain jacket/pants
- [ ] Thermal layers
- [ ] Wicked/quick-dry clothing
- [ ] Loose-fitting shirts
- [ ] Loose-fitting pants
- [ ] Hiking pants/shorts
- [ ] Short-sleeved/sleeveless shirts
- [ ] Full winter gear
  - ....
  - ....
  - ....
- [ ] Leisurewear
- [ ] Beachwear
- [ ] Hiking shoes
- [ ] Athletic shoes
- [ ] Water shoes
- [ ] Sandals/flip-flops
- [ ] Neck gaiter
- [ ] Sun hat/cap
- [ ] Stocking cap
- [ ] Socks + extra pair
- [ ] Undergarments
- [ ] Gloves/mittens
- [ ] ....
- [ ] ....
- [ ] ....
- [ ] ....
- [ ] ....
- [ ] ....
- [ ] ....

OUTDOOR GEAR

- [ ] Hiking poles
- [ ] Tent
- [ ] Sleeping bag
- [ ] Sleeping pad
- [ ] Pillow
- [ ] Shade tent
- [ ] Emergency space blanket
- [ ] Tarp
- [ ] Daypack
- [ ] Headlamp(s)
- [ ] Lantern(s)
- [ ] Water filter & iodine tablets
- [ ] Large refillable water jug
- [ ] Portable stove
- [ ] Hot beverage thermos
- [ ] Nylon hammock
- [ ] Throw blanket
- [ ] Reusable dishes/cutlery
- [ ] Hand warmers
- [ ] ....
- [ ] ....
- [ ] ....
- [ ] ....
- [ ] ....
- [ ] ....
- [ ] ....
- [ ] ....
- [ ] ....
- [ ] ....

FOOD & DRINK

- [ ] Water
- [ ] Refillable water bottle
- [ ] Energy drinks with electrolytes
- [ ] Protein-packed snacks
- [ ] Salty, easy-to-digest snacks
- [ ] Dehydrated food
- [ ] No-cook food items
- [ ] ....
- [ ] ....
- [ ] ....
- [ ] ....
- [ ] ....
- [ ] ....
- [ ] ....
- [ ] ....
- [ ] ....
- [ ] ....
- [ ] ....
- [ ] ....
- [ ] ....
- [ ] ....
- [ ] ....

PARK-SPECIFIC

- [ ] *The National Parks Journal*!
- [ ] Permits
- [ ] Guidebooks
- [ ] Park map
- [ ] ....
- [ ] ....
- [ ] ....
- [ ] ....
- [ ] ....
- [ ] ....
- [ ] ....

MISCELLANEOUS

- [ ] Duct tape
- [ ] Multipurpose tool
- [ ] Knife
- [ ] Scissors
- [ ] Can opener
- [ ] Matches/lighter/firestarter
- [ ] Hatchet
- [ ] Whistle
- [ ] Bandana
- [ ] Quick-dry towels
- [ ] Waterproof bags
- [ ] Ziplock bags
- [ ] Trash bags
- [ ] Paper towels
- [ ] Bear can
- [ ] Binoculars
- [ ] Deck of cards/games
- [ ] Driver's license, registration, insurance, etc.
- [ ] Spare tire/jack
- [ ] Wiper blades
- [ ] Small amount of cash
- [ ] ....
- [ ] ....
- [ ] ....
- [ ] ....
- [ ] ....
- [ ] ....
- [ ] ....
- [ ] ....
- [ ] ....
- [ ] ....
- [ ] ....
- [ ] ....
- [ ] ....
- [ ] ....

PERSONALIZED LIST

- [ ] ....
- [ ] ....
- [ ] ....
- [ ] ....
- [ ] ....
- [ ] ....
- [ ] ....
- [ ] ....
- [ ] ....
- [ ] ....
- [ ] ....

TO BUY

- [ ] ....
- [ ] ....
- [ ] ....
- [ ] ....
- [ ] ....
- [ ] ....
- [ ] ....
- [ ] ....
- [ ] ....

ADDITIONAL NOTES

RECORD YOUR TRIP!

Park name: ....

State/territory: ....

Dates visited: ....

Nearby sites visited: ....

ARROWHEAD RATING!

- 5 — Epic & life-changing experience
- 4 — Want to learn everything about this park!
- 3 — See why this place is so special
- 2 — Happy I went and had some good times
- 1 — Once and done!

FAVORITE CAMPSITE OR LODGING: ....
....

PEAK EXPERIENCE: ....
....

FAVORITE ADVENTURE: ....
....

FAVORITE LOCATION: ....
....

FAVORITE PHOTO: ....
....

BEST WILDLIFE SIGHTING: ....
....

FUN THING(S) I LEARNED ABOUT THE PARK: ....
....

INTERESTING PEOPLE MET ALONG MY JOURNEY: --

VALUABLE RESOURCE(S) DISCOVERED ALONG THE WAY: --------------------------------------

----

FOOD I COULDN'T LIVE WITHOUT: --

THE BIGGEST CHALLENGE I FACED: ---

I WAS MOST PREPARED WHEN: --

WISH I KNEW BEFORE I WENT: ---

WISH I WOULD HAVE BROUGHT: ---

MOST USEFUL PIECE OF GEAR: ---

MOST VALUABLE TOOL: --

MOST USEFUL PIECE OF ADVICE: ---

TIPS FOR OTHER TRAVELERS: --

ADDITIONAL NOTES: --

INDEX

About the Author

Stefanie Payne is a content strategist supporting NASA human spaceflight at the agency's headquarters in Washington, DC. She also writes about adventures on Earth, with articles and photographs appearing on the Travel Channel, along with blogs for *The National Geographic Society* and *Lonely Planet*. In 2016, she took on The Greatest American Road Trip, documenting fifty-nine US national parks in fifty-two weeks. Learn more at TheGreatestRoadTrip.com and follow along @iStefPayne on *Twitter* and *Instagram*.